D1015653

The Love *R*esponse

Eva M. Selhub, M.D.

with *Divina Infusino*

YOUR PRESCRIPTION TO
TURN OFF FEAR, ANGER, AND ANXIETY
TO ACHIEVE VIBRANT HEALTH AND
TRANSFORM YOUR LIFE

BALLANTINE BOOKS • NEW YORK

The author has changed the names and personal characteristics of individuals discussed in *The Love Response* in order to conceal their identities. Any resemblance to persons, living or dead, is entirely coincidental and unintentional.

The material in this book is supplied for informational purposes only and is not meant to take the place of a doctor's advice. No book can replace the diagnostic expertise and medical advice of a trusted professional. Please be certain to consult with your health care provider before making any decisions that affect your health.

Published in the United States by Ballantine Books,
an imprint of The Random House Publishing Group,
a division of Random House, Inc., New York.

BALLANTINE and colophon are registered trademarks of Random House, Inc.

The Love Response, the SHIELD, and Active Belief System are
registered trademarks of Eva M. Selhub, M.D.

For a complimentary audio download of *The Love Response*
meditations and exercises please go to www.audible.com/loveresponse.
An unabridged audio edition of *The Love Response,* read by the author,
is available wherever audiobooks are sold.
Produced and published by Brilliance Audio, Inc.
Also available for download from www.audible.com.

LIBRARY OF CONGRESS CATALOGING-IN-PUBLICATION DATA
Selhub, Eva M.
The love response : your prescription to turn off fear, anger, and anxiety
to achieve vibrant health and transform your life / Eva M. Selhub
with Divina Infusino.
p.   cm.
Includes bibliographical references and index.
ISBN 978-0-345-50652-8 (hardcover : alk. paper)
e-ISBN 978-0-345-51281-9
1. Love.   2. Fear.   3. Stress (Psychology)   4. Health.
I. Infusino, Divina.   II. Title.
BF575.L8S45 2009
177'.7—dc22   2008044426

Printed in the United States of America on acid-free paper

www.ballantinebooks.com

2 4 6 8 9 7 5 3 1

FIRST EDITION

Book design by Mary A. Wirth

For my loving family:
Jacob, Shirley, Julie, Eliya, and
Maia (papaya) Selhub

CONTENTS

INTRODUCTION

Through years of work with thousands of patients, I've learned one unequivocal truth about human health: just because a disease enters the body does not mean its symptoms will manifest.

For most of my medical career, I have sought out the differences between a body that can fight disease and one that cannot, between one person prone to health and another to illness.

What I found out is startling:

THE BIGGEST OBSTACLES TO GOOD HEALTH ARE STRESS AND FEAR.

and

THE ANTIDOTE TO STRESS AND FEAR IS LOVE.

The Love Response is built on these premises.

My big moment of insight into stress and love did not occur in a clinical setting or through scientific means. It happened in a hospital delivery room the day my niece, Maia, was born.

On April 16, 2002, when I snipped her umbilical cord and held her for the first time, all my worries, fears, problems, and stress seemed to dissolve, and for a moment the world stood still. As Maia grew, I experienced this feeling again and again whenever I was with her. Then one day, while the three-year-old Maia rested on my chest, she lifted her head to look up at me, gently swept some hair off my face, and said, "Auntie, I love you." There it was again: all my worries and fears evaporated in that moment.

I thought, "How can this be? Time can never stand still, so why does it feel this way?" I've had this experience other times too—when I'd gazed at a beautiful sunset, listened to music, or bonded deeply to someone or something. It happens when I am in a state of awe or appreciation. What I realized was that in moments like this, we connect to the rhythm and flow of life and the gates of infinite possibilities open up before our eyes and in our hearts. Time doesn't stand still; rather, *we* are still.

As the medical director of the Mind/Body Medical Institute at the Beth Israel Deaconess Medical Center, I have witnessed the restorative power of the "Relaxation Response," the series of biochemical events that occur in the body when you are in a state of deep relaxation most commonly brought on by the practice of meditation, tai chi, qi gong, or any other repetitive focus. I know how initiating the Relaxation Response enables patients to better handle stress, find wellness, and develop a belief that they can stay well in the future. Years of scientific research bears this out. Practiced regularly, the Relaxation Response reduces blood pressure, migraines, heart rate, muscle tension, and other symptoms of stress. In short, the Relaxation Response improves health.

In that one moment with Maia, I realized that a short burst of love had the same positive effects on my body as a long session of meditation. It seemed that love triggered a similar positive biochemistry as the Relaxation Response. But instead of requiring that I sit alone in a contemplative state for twenty minutes or more, love could achieve the same, even more predictable result in mere seconds.

I spent the next three years combing through research studies supporting this idea. As I pieced together the data, it revealed a scientific truth: when you experience love in any form—love for another, for yourself, for spirit or something greater than yourself—you are healing your body. Why? Because love takes you out of the state of resistance that causes stress—the stress that lays the groundwork for disease. With love, you experience less stress and fear every day. Of course you should see your doctor when you are concerned about your health, but with less stress and fear, you can be happier and healthier for the rest of your life.

So how can you bring the healing powers of love into your life? The Love Response will show you step-by-step, easy-to-use techniques that will keep you on a path to long-term wellness and well-being each and every day.

THE LOVE RESPONSE

The Love Response gives you the tools to heal your body from the ravages of stress and fear that most everyone constantly endures. It shows you how to build a life based on love in all its forms and how to change your thoughts and feelings of dread and pain to relief and joy in moments.

Each person has physical, emotional, psychological, and spiritual strengths as well as weaknesses. Health is not an end result but a life-long process of discovering how to support your strengths and lever-age your weaknesses as opportunities for growth. The Love Response gives you the tools for this process, so you can tune into your instincts in your own way, on your own timeline, and in harmony with your individual needs, goals, and motivations.

The Love Response enables you to build a life that reflects who you really are—a being meant to live in the dynamics of love, with bodies that can heal disease and sustain a lifetime of health.

MY STORY

Long before Maia was born, however, the pieces of the Love Response puzzle began to reveal themselves to me. Indeed, I learned the power of the Love Response through personal experience: I was my own first patient.

At age twenty-eight, I was a doctor on my way to specializing in pulmonary medicine. Then, in literally one moment, everything in my life changed forever.

On a beautiful June day, just weeks away from completing my second year of residency, I had been working for twenty hours straight in a Boston hospital's intensive care unit (ICU). All ten ICU beds were occupied by gravely ill patients.

At 2 a.m., exhausted, two interns and I shuffled to the call room.

I had just dozed off when the emergency buzzer awakened me. A patient's central IV line had fallen out and needed replacing. Being superwoman, I let the interns sleep and went to handle the problem myself.

I made my way to the comatose patient's bedside and located the errant IV line. I had just managed to insert the IV needle into the patient's vein when suddenly, without any warning, he began coughing and bucking. The needle slipped out and punctured my finger, right through my glove, exposing me to the blood of a patient who had full-blown AIDS and hepatitis C.

My mind raced in panic:

"Oh, God! I've been stuck! Look at all this blood . . . I have to wash it off. If only I could cut my finger off now.

"Should I tell someone? . . . I don't want to tell anyone. I feel like a fool, like a failure. How stupid! What will people say . . . what will they think? They'll think that I'm not good enough to be doing these procedures.

"Maybe if I squeeze hard enough, all the blood will come out . . . If only I could chop this finger off! Keep rinsing . . . get some ammonia, alcohol . . . something.

"Should I tell someone? I need to tell someone. Who? I don't think I'll be able to get through this alone."

Before this moment, I had never experienced the threat of a real illness, either physical or psychological, that I could not handle on my own. I prided myself on being robust, self-sufficient, motivated, and capable. Like many women, I strove for perfection. To be anything less was not good enough and would mean that *I* wasn't good enough. Asking for help was not part of the agreement I made with myself. Asking for help would imply weakness, vulnerability, shame.

Now, in seconds, all those presumptions crumbled. I met my mortality face-to-face and everything that I had been striving toward became irrelevant and obsolete. For the first time in my life, I felt completely out of control of my body and health. I needed to ask for help. In one stroke, I felt like a victim.

I did tell someone; I did seek help. That night, I consulted with an infectious-disease physician about the HIV needle stick. "High-risk exposure" was all I heard. To my mind, this meant I was going to die.

The attending physician attempted to comfort me with statistics.

All I could do was cry. No reassurance could stop the fear and frenzy of thoughts raging in my head.

The next day, I started an experimental regimen of anti-HIV drugs. I also decided to tell my family, which for me was no easy feat. I had always seen myself as "the strong one," the one everyone else depended upon. I felt ashamed for "failing," for being vulnerable, for being human and making a huge mistake. Telling my family would bring them pain and me humiliation. I loathed the idea of worrying them.

Nonetheless, there we sat, my father, mother, sister, and brother in my small living room, holding one another and crying. From that moment on, they rarely left my side.

In the ensuing six weeks, I grew anemic from the medication I took, experienced profound fatigue, and suffered through excruciating bouts of abdominal pain. I now understood what it was like to be ill, anxious, distressed, relying on the help of others, and feeling totally out of control.

The needle stick marked the beginning of a six-month downward spiral of personal disasters, including the death of my grandfather, the death of my dog, a smear campaign from someone I had never met who tried to destroy my reputation with the medical board, a fire that raged through my apartment, leaving nothing but a black pit of ash, and, finally, the hospitalization of my father for a heart attack.

Even though I was eventually pronounced HIV-free, the strain of this six-month period did me in. I had experienced too much loss in too little time. I shut down. I could not smile, think, or remember. I was supposed to take my medical boards very soon, but I had no desire to study. I had fallen into a dark abyss and couldn't see a way out.

As much as I wanted to give up on life, life—in the form of my friends, family, and colleagues—did not give up on me. They saw something in me that was worth loving. They rallied around me, forcing me to attend social events when all I wanted to do was stay home and hide. They stayed with me when I felt alone, reminding me that every day holds new hope and possibilities.

I managed to step back into life, complete my residency, and embark on a career of primary care medicine. But I wasn't done battling my demons yet.

Less than two years later, in the midst of seeing sixteen patients in a four-hour period, I began experiencing anxiety attacks. Teetering on the verge of hyperventilating, I forced myself to take deep breaths in between patients just to stop my heart from racing.

I had never experienced anything like a panic attack before. Why was this happening? I had a litany of reasons:

> I hated my job.
> I lacked enough time to connect with my patients or
>   colleagues.
> I missed my friends who had moved away to other cities.
> I felt abandoned and alone.
> I felt trapped by working nonstop, then fighting traffic
>   to arrive to an empty home and an empty life, only to
>   have the cycle start up again the next day.

These were all true. But I didn't think that any of these problems—even in combination—could account for something as extreme as panic attacks. I had to look deeper.

I found that I hated my job because I felt manipulated and disrespected by the system.

I found that I missed my friends so much because I was still deeply brokenhearted about a relationship that had left me feeling betrayed and dejected.

I found that I felt trapped by my life because nothing in my existence gave me meaning or validation.

As I contemplated my predicament and became quiet internally, I saw a consistent pattern: no matter the circumstances, no matter the people involved—my friends, family, work, relationships—I could not get enough love and recognition. In truth, I did not love myself, and because of that, I did not believe that someone else could love me.

This realization blew me away. I knew I needed to change this distorted belief, so I began to repeat slowly under my breath: "I love myself, I love myself." Saying these words—even though I didn't really believe them at the time—seemed to relieve my anxiety.

I repeated those words again to myself whenever a panic attack reared its ugly head. *Hold on, Eva. This physical reaction is a reflection of something that isn't right internally. What is the universe telling you that you are not listening to? What are you reacting to? If you truly loved yourself, what would you want?*

I tried making a list of what I wanted, but all I could think about was what I didn't want, so I started from there. It was a long list, but soon after, I matched my "don't wants" with my "do wants" and discovered that I wanted something else, something better than what I had worked so hard to achieve.

I wanted to do something I enjoyed and believed in.

I wanted to work in a different kind of medical environment, one that did not only treat patients once they were acutely ill but kept them from getting sick at all.

I envisioned a friendly, supportive work environment, where I could spend an hour with each patient.

I wanted peace in my heart and stillness in my spirit.

A month later I quit my job.

I began intense studies in alternative medicine, Chinese medicine, and energy work. I learned how to align with and value myself. I learned to allow the people and pets around me to love me, which, in turn, taught me how to love myself. I learned to give and receive love to something higher than myself, to Spirit.

DEVELOPING THE LOVE RESPONSE

Through all my study in alternative medicine, I tried whatever I learned on myself first and then taught my patients. I began my consulting practice as an integrative health specialist working with patients from all walks of life suffering from many different diseases. I used Western medicine to treat their acute problems and alleviate the symptoms of illness (which can cause fear) and Eastern medicine to address the actual causes of disease.

When I taught my patients the simple techniques I had learned to access love quickly, their emotional and physical problems improved more rapidly than anyone could have anticipated.

This was all beginning to make sense to me just about the time my niece, Maia, was born. Holding her that first day in the hospital and each time thereafter, it became clear to me that there was a profound link between cuddling a baby and banishing stress from the body. Along with years of clinical practice, that insight yielded the Love Response, a wellness program based in science that neutralizes the harmful effects of stress and fear on your body and restores your natural balance of health and well-being.

The Love Response is founded on one universal truth: love heals. Not in a greeting card, positive psychology kind of way—although that's certainly part of it—but at a biochemical, physiological level that actually makes your body well again.

I know it can be difficult to wrap your mind around the reality that love can actually heal the physical body, not just emotional wounds. At my first session with patients, I explain the process of the Love Response and the words out of their mouths are invariably the same: "Does this actually work?" Having seen this process heal myself and my patients time and again, I tell you what I tell them: "If it didn't work, I wouldn't have a job." And I've been honing and practicing this method for more than a decade.

Even though it takes work to break free of the cycle of fear and turn to love, it is actually not hard work. It involves waking up a bit, noticing how you live and how you react to challenges, real or imagined. It involves becoming aware of your body, its needs, and how it feels. It means *choosing* to love yourself, taking care of yourself as well as others, and taking the steps that help you become more resilient to life's challenges.

The next chapter will introduce you to the cause of most illnesses from which we commonly suffer: Fear. When Franklin D. Roosevelt said, "The only thing we have to fear is fear itself," little did he know that he was verbalizing a universal medical truth. Even today, most Western doctors have no idea how inextricably entwined illness and fear are.

I welcome you to open your minds to a revolutionary way of healing your body and your life.

—Eva Selhub, M.D.

The Love Response

1

FEAR

The Ultimate Silent Killer

I magine you are lost. You have no map, and no GPS, and your mobile phone is out of range. What are your thoughts and feelings? "I am going to be late. Where am I? What am I going to do?" You are likely to feel out of control and anxious.

When you meet an obstacle for which you think you are unprepared, when you feel you lack the resources you need to cope with a situation, your body automatically undergoes a series of biochemical reactions in which you experience stress and fear.

At its most primitive level, fear keeps human beings out of the mouths of wild animals and away from dark, dangerous places. It also goads us out of our comfort zone so we can experience new things, and grow and evolve as people.

Fear gets us out into the world. It drives us to learn, achieve, and acquire knowledge. Fear creates a sense of urgency to fix what is not right. Fear has pushed society to overcome tuberculosis and certain cancers, to fly through the sky, and to take care of basic survival needs such as food, water, and shelter. On a purely physical level, fear prompts our bodies to heal wounds, survive traumas, and run from danger.

Go back to the example of being lost without a map. Fear could incite you to muster the resources you have and work hard to find a solution. In this case, fear results in a productive response and action. Once you find your way again, your anxiety and the adrenaline that helped you to safety usually subside and your body returns to balance.

Now imagine you have been lost in the woods alone for hours. You have nothing with you but the small lunch and bottle of water you packed for what was supposed to be a short hike. In this scenario, you may be so unnerved that you stop thinking clearly, go beyond the kind of adrenaline rush that might help you, and move instead into panic mode.

In this case, fear and stress are no longer helpful but harmful—they override your body's normal functions and send your mind into a place where you no longer operate rationally. This is just one dangerous side effect of unchecked fear, and unless you can get it under control, it will be difficult for you to find your way to safety.

Fear and stress are necessary and natural parts of life when they function as intended—as a temporary, short-lived state that raises blood pressure, quickens breath, and pumps cortisol and adrenaline into the system to keep us out of harm's way. Fear and stress damage your health when they strike too often or linger too long, a problem you certainly have suffered from if you live in the modern world.

Today, rest and quiet time are a luxury. We set an alarm to wake us up in the morning so that we rarely sleep until our bodies are rested. We gulp down breakfast and rush to work, where we're constantly under pressure to perform more and faster. Ten minutes for lunch? Oh, just skip it—who needs to eat? After eight to ten hours of madness, it's hurry home for a couple of hours of quality time, by yourself or with your family, before going to bed and starting the whole cycle over again the next day.

Oh, yes, and then comes the weekend, filled with shopping and mowing and cleaning and baseball and ballet and social and cultural events to attend. Who has time to rest? I'm exhausted just thinking about it!

Our twenty-first-century lifestyles keep us operating in a constant state of anxiety and fear. It might not be active or obvious, but your fear is idling so high all the time that it does precipitate what I call the Fear Response. Whether it is gridlock on the morning commute, a disagreement at the office, a migraine, or a divorce, the body responds the same way: it locks into a cycle of fear symptoms such as tight muscles, poor digestion, a racing heart, anxiety, and or inability to sleep.

The problem is that we usually do not run off the adrenaline and cortisol that builds up in our bloodstream as our ancestors did when they spotted a lion and hightailed it to safety. Instead, the physical effects of the Fear Response course through our systems day in and day out as we sit in front of a crashed computer or fume at a customer service rep over the phone. Fear builds on itself until it becomes a biofeedback loop we cannot turn off.

Eventually, it overwhelms our minds and bodies and results in what I call "negative physiology," a biochemical imbalance that is at the root of almost all diseases.

Fear and its corollaries of anger, shame, and loneliness are sometimes normal and healthy emotions. Too much of them for too long can kill you—literally.

The Physiology of Fear

Science shows that fear affects every aspect of your body and mind, including your brain function, immune system, mental and emotional states, and propensity toward illness. How?

The Fear Response stimulates the amygdala-hippocampus complex (AHC), your emotional response center and the primitive part of the brain, often called "the lizard brain." The lizard brain directs the emotions or behaviors that are necessary for survival of the species, such as fear and aggression. The lizard brain also stores the memory of any given negative experience or threat so that you can react even faster to it in the future.[1]

Stimulation of the lizard brain triggers a cascade of events, culminating in the production of hormones and peptides, such as cortisol and adrenaline, that cause physical changes in the body. At the same time, changes occur in the brain that prevent you from doing any complex problem solving—you actually revert to a more primitive being whose main goal is physical self-preservation.[2]

The Physical Changes

To best understand the Fear Response, imagine this: a lion is chasing you. Or, to use a more modern-day example: you're working on an extremely tight deadline and your company's success depends on your finishing a project and finishing it well. Is it a good time to take a nap? Ah, no. The Fear Response eliminates any chance of that because it sends adrenaline coursing through the brain to keep you alert, aroused, and hypervigilant. It is not a good time to reproduce either, so your reproductive system shuts down (hormonal mayhem!). It is not such a good time to forage for food, so your digestive system shuts off. You might experience contractions of the esophagus or slowing down of the intestines (peristalsis). Since you need to be strong enough to fight or run, the blood flow to the brain and large muscle groups increases and the muscles themselves tense, specifically in the lower back, neck, and shoulders. The fists and jaw jut forward so that your face appears threatening—just imagine the face you make when someone tries to take your parking spot!

All this activity requires fuel, so the body initiates catabolism, a process that takes nutrients out of the system so you can use them for energy. With catabolism, the bones break down to release calcium and magnesium, muscles break down to provide protein, fat breaks down to produce glucose. To get more oxygen for energy, you breathe faster. If you are cut or wounded, the immune system rushes to the rescue to clot the blood if necessary. It sends white blood cells out to fight infection or starts allergic reactions to keep out foreign substances. Meanwhile, to get the fuel and immune cells quickly to the places where they are needed, your heart rate and blood pressure rise.

SYMPTOMS OF THE FEAR RESPONSE

- *Brain:* You are hyperalert, unable to sleep, anxious.
- *Muscles:* You feel tense, especially in your neck, back, shoulders, and jaw.
- *Reproduction:* You miss your period or have light menstruation or low libido or sperm count.
- *Gastrointestinal tract:* You are constipated or have loose stools, heartburn, or cramping.
- *Blood flow:* You have cold hands and feet.
- *Heart:* Your heart races and pumps harder and your blood pressure rises.
- *Lungs:* You breathe faster or more shallowly.
- *Immune system:* Your white blood cells get ready for a possible attack, causing inflammation.

Check It Out!

You can see for yourself how the Fear Response affects your body. Try following these steps.

- Close your eyes.
- Think about a stressful or upsetting experience. Try to imagine that you are there again.
- Pay attention to your breathing.
- Things to notice:

  — Are you holding your breath?
  — Are you breathing more shallowly or faster?
  — Do you notice your chest feels tighter?
  — Do you notice if your shoulders may be falling forward?
  — Do you feel a "stuck" feeling in your upper chest or throat?

- Now open your eyes and set the intention to go through your day, paying attention to when and if you hold your breath and the associated circumstances. Notice any other bodily sensations or feelings that occur when you are experiencing stress.

Most of you will find that you hold your breath during stressful situations or even when thinking about them. In fact, you might notice that you are tensing your shoulders or holding your breath most of the day. If so, it's time to wake up—you're killing yourself!

Fear and Health

The Fear Response is like a fire—beneficial when it cooks your food but harmful if it is not extinguished. If the Fear Response continues too long or unregulated, the body stays in a constant state of stress and pathological problems inevitably arise, including increases in blood pressure and thickening of and tears in blood vessel walls. Excess production of fatty acids and blood sugar may lead to deposits in these tears and formation of atherosclerotic plaques, eventually resulting in heart disease and stroke. The combination of excessive adrenaline and cortisol production and high levels of insulin released from the pancreas in response to elevated glucose levels may eventually lead to insulin-resistant diabetes and other metabolic disorders such as high cholesterol, especially when your diet is rich in simple sugars and/or carbohydrates. As cortisol levels rise, fat is deposited in different areas of your body to store fuel—that's why you develop that lovely spare tire around the waist.

In the past, when large, scary animals threatened your life, the Fear Response helped you either fight or run away. The Fear Response subsided when the danger was over. Today, however, when your brain reacts to a social or psychological stressor as if a lion is close on your heels, your physical activity response is more likely to involve watching TV or working on the computer than sprinting for the nearest tree. You do not use up the energy generated by the Fear Response, so your body deposits it, storing it in your fat cells instead. These fat cells then secrete the same inflammatory cells that turn on the Fear Response, causing your body to produce more cortisol and therefore deposit more fat. Get the picture?

FEAR RESPONSE OVERLOAD LEADS TO[3]

- High blood pressure
- Heart disease and strokes
- Infertility and sexual dysfunction
- Muscle tension and pain
- Arthritis and other inflammatory problems
- Obesity
- Memory loss and poor concentration
- High glucose and high cholesterol
- Increased risk for osteoporosis
- Gastrointestinal problems
- Weakened immune system

Chronically elevated levels of cortisol, inflammatory cells, and adrenaline can also lead to many pathological problems in the brain, including:

- Increases in free radical and oxidative stress leading to memory loss
- Changes in brain chemicals such as a rise in neuropeptides that

increase the desire to overeat and decrease the impulse for physical activity

- Decreases in serotonin which lead to cravings for sweets, fats, and other junk foods
- Decreases in the brain's ability to use glucose so that you lose brainpower

Interestingly, when you experience chronic stress, the body uses serotonin in high amounts to keep the stress response active. Meanwhile, the stress produces cortisol, which inhibits absorption of tryptophan, the amino acid precursor of serotonin, thus further reducing total serotonin levels. Low serotonin may lead to a variety of mood disorders such as depression or sleep disorders and produce cravings for junk or "comfort" food, prolonging the vicious cycle.

Elevated adrenaline levels may also lead to constant muscle tension and/or inflammation, instigating various pain and musculoskeletal disorders. Lack of blood flow to the gastrointestinal (GI) tract and changes in hydrochloric acid secretion may result in peptic ulcer disease, irritable bowel syndrome, inflammatory bowel disease, and other gastrointestinal disorders. Of course, the more your body breaks down, the more you worry. The cycle perpetuates itself, as with my patient Cynthia.

 CYNTHIA: *Fear Begets More Fear*

Cynthia, a very active sixty-two-year-old woman, complained to me of her heart racing, upper back and neck pain, and insomnia. She described herself as a "doer and a fixer." She was constantly on the go; her skills and capabilities were always in demand. She had little patience for ignorance, and when she wanted something done, she did it herself. She felt that when a job was left up to others, it did not get done properly. She was frustrated because she could not do the things she had formerly enjoyed, such as being physically active, because her pain or her racing heart got in the way. Worrying about her health and the following day's tasks kept her awake at night.

Cynthia admitted that she had always been a "worrier," and she believed that her constant vigilance had made her successful. She had spent her life fretting about what "might happen" and doing everything in her power to ensure that it didn't. Now her focus had turned to her health, and unlike some of the other tasks that she worried about in the past, she could not control this. In fact, the more she worried about her health, the more her symptoms worsened, creating more fear. Her heart raced more, and she had a harder time sleeping. The more she didn't sleep, the more pain she experienced.

Cynthia learned the techniques that you will read about in this book. She discovered that when she consciously and deliberately deactivated her Fear Response, her heart raced less, her body aches decreased, and her sleep improved. She was well on her way to taking her health back.

Twenty-Four-Hour Security: The Immune System

When the Fear Response goes unchecked, our body's security patrol, the immune system, especially takes a beating. As the Fear Response stays active, cortisol and adrenaline levels remain high and the immune system shuts down, making you prone to infection and possibly tumors or cancer. At the same time, more inflammation occurs, which increases the chance of developing inflammatory disorders. Current research shows that an inflammatory component exists in almost all disorders known to traditional Western medicine, from arthritis, autoimmune disorders, and allergies to diabetes, obesity, depression, and cardiovascular disease.[4]

What You Should Know About the Immune System

You are born with only one part of your immune system. As you grow, you develop the rest of it. This more sophisticated portion of your immune system has two parts that work together as your twenty-four-hour security system: the part that works mostly during the day ("daytime security") and the part that works mostly at night ("nighttime security"). Daytime security is responsible for protecting you against larger organisms and the things you may come into contact with during the day. It kills certain bacteria and prompts allergic reactions against foreign substances.

Nighttime security protects you against smaller organisms that may invade your cells at night, such as viruses or tumors. The daytime and nighttime security systems communicate with each other through messengers called cytokines. The cytokines from each system tell the other to take a break while the other is working.

So what?

Normally, at night, cortisol levels are low. When the Fear Response continues for too long, however, cortisol levels remain high even at night, especially if you are not sleeping well. Nighttime security is very sensitive to cortisol. When your levels of cortisol are too high, nighttime security weakens, reducing your defenses against tumors or viruses. It also stops producing its messenger cells or cytokines, and therefore daytime security doesn't get the message to turn itself off. Daytime security can then overreact to substances in the environment, so you develop allergies. Or it becomes hypervigilant to the point that it attacks your own body, resulting in inflammation or autoimmune disorders.

Burnout

Sometimes the immune system is so overworked that it grows hypersensitive and overreactive, as if it had a mind of its own. The communication between the mind and body turns erratic, becoming more like the game of telephone—messages get distorted and even changed. When this occurs, your Fear Response has been so overactivated that your body's systems experience "burnout."

What happens to an engine when a car travels at 120 miles per hour for a long time? The engine overheats and burns out. All the systems in that car stop functioning and communicating with one another. This can also happen to your body. For some reason—and the theories for why this is vary—the Fear Response itself, the engine that's been powering your body, burns out. Rather than becoming hyperalert, the reverse happens and profound fatigue and a state of low arousal ensue. The brain loses communication with the immune cells, so irritability and inflammation increase. The adrenal glands, tired from overworking, cannot produce adequate cortisol. The hypothalamus also lacks the energy or ability to initiate an adequate Fear Response.

Clinical conditions that reflect an underactive Fear Response include chronic fatigue syndrome, early menopause, hypothyroidism, fibromyalgia, and rheumatoid arthritis. In these conditions, cortisol levels are usually low and the immune cells are off and running, doing their own thing. Many individuals suffering from these disorders, in fact, develop hypersensitivity reactions to foods, chemicals, and other substances that they often need for daily living. Many of these clinical conditions often have no rhyme or reason and baffle the Western medical community.

TYPICAL BURNOUT CONDITIONS[5]

- Chronic fatigue
- Rheumatoid arthritis
- Autoimmune disorders
- Hypersensitivity/allergies
- Worsening symptoms of menopause (hot flashes, low libido, insomnia, brain fog, etc.)
- Fibromyalgia
- Depression

 HELEN: *Burned Out and Tired*

Helen was thirty-seven when she came to see me. She had a history of hypothyroidism (underactive thyroid) and depression and was moderately overweight. She informed me that she had recently been diagnosed with chronic fatigue syndrome. While happy to finally have a diagnosis, Helen felt very distressed about being labeled with a condition that had no "cure" or known cause. She was frustrated because she used to be a high-functioning individual, with a successful career, a rigorous exercise regime, a stable relationship, and a compulsively neat home. During her divorce several years earlier, she had come down with the flu and "never recovered." Her symptoms included aching joints and muscles and an overwhelming sense of fatigue. Any kind of challenging situation made her feel worse. Exercise aggravated her symptoms. Deadlines at work exacerbated her fatigue. She craved carbohydrates, ate and slept more, exercised less, gained weight that she couldn't lose, and could not keep an orderly house.

I asked Helen about her childhood. It turned out that her father had been an alcoholic, and she had lost contact with him in her teens, when her parents divorced. Her mother was loving and supportive, although she suffered from depression and anxiety. I explained to Helen that the abandonment and fear she had experienced in her relationship with her father and the physiology she had inherited from both her parents had set her Fear Response into hyperreactive mode at a young age. Children of alcoholic parents never know what to expect of the adult, who is unpredictable in his or her behavior. They live in constant fear, remain hyperalert, and strive to be perfect, so as not to upset the parent. I asked her to notice how her entire life she had conquered life's challenges with hypervigilance.

I explained to Helen that perhaps she had been on "overdrive" all her life, so that the ensuing trauma of her marriage/divorce and then illness had caused her Fear Response to "burn out." What she perceived as threatening had not changed, nor had her emotions, which meant her Fear Response continued unabated. But rather than being alert and aroused, she became pathologically fatigued.

Something to think about: trillions of cells make up your body. Unhealthy cells—cancer cells, mutated cells, cells with parasites, tired cells, and so on—are bound to exist in the mix. When your immune system is functioning well, it gets rid of these "bad" cells or creates security walls around them so that they do not harm the body, especially if they do not accumulate in large numbers. But your immune cells, like the rest of your body, can do only so much.

Like loyal employees, your immune cells need a clean space to work in. They require respect, good compensation, and time off for good work. They need good instruction and leadership. They change depending on what you eat, how much you move about, and how much you sleep. They alter depending on your thoughts, emotions, and how other people treat you.

MARYBETH: *Fear Hurts*

Marybeth was forty-four years old when she came to see me for an annual checkup. She complained of poor sleep, hot flashes, frequent tension headaches, irritability, and decreased libido. She did not believe she was depressed, however. She had a history of breast cancer and was still taking tamoxifen as part of the long-term chemotherapy protocol. Unfortunately, tamoxifen, a medication used to treat certain types of breast cancer, was causing many of the side effects she was experiencing. Marybeth wanted to "be fixed." She wanted to get back to being "normal," "like I was before the breast cancer." I suggested that she try the programs at Mind/Body Medical Institute, in which she would learn some self-care techniques to help her feel better, but she refused to try the treatment I was offering. Marybeth just wanted me to prescribe a drug that would miraculously cure her symptoms. I knew there was no such magic pill and told her the real cure for her problems was something else. She didn't want to hear that.

So as she was not a candidate for hormone replacement therapy, I tried every remedy in the "traditional medical book," to no avail. She saw me about once a month for approximately six months, her frustration mounting with each visit, as no "cure" was found. She never wanted to discuss her breast cancer diagnosis, insisting that it was "no big deal." She would say, "I didn't miss a day of work during treatment. I didn't have fear around it then, and I don't have fear around it now."

About six months later, when Marybeth came for yet another visit, she began crying. "I woke up this morning and realized that I just survived breast cancer. It's the first time the full impact of it really hit me," she said. "I'm scared. What can I do?" At last! Marybeth's condition was associated with a significant amount of emotional upset—feelings of anxiety, isolation, and being out of control—that had worsened her symptoms. When I again offered to introduce her to the techniques I knew would help her, this time she didn't hesitate.

Six months after this emotional breakthrough, she walked into the clinic with a smile on her face and exclaimed tearfully, "Thank you! You've changed my life, I feel great. I have no more hot flashes. I sleep like a baby. My headaches are gone, my libido is great, and, by the way, my husband wants to thank you!" I was moved but very aware that I had done nothing to "cure" Marybeth. I had given her neither a medication nor an operation. I had not taken her off tamoxifen, the drug responsible for most of her symptoms, because her breast cancer therapy protocol required that she stay on it. But by showing her techniques to control her Fear Response, I had given her a way to heal herself, to leave the world of negative physiology and take back control of her own health and well-being.

Like Marybeth, you have the ability to shift out of your Fear Response and change your health. Your first step is to notice if you have symptoms of an overactive Fear Response. The more symptoms you have, the more likely your life is out of balance.

FEAR QUESTIONNAIRE

The following questionnaire will help you assess how out of control fear is in your life. Notice how frequently your Fear Response is activated and how well your mind and body handle it. The more symptoms or problems you have, the more out of control your Fear Response is.

Rate the following questions as follows:

Always true: 4
More often than not true: 3
Rarely true: 2
Not true: 1

Take your time in answering these questions as truthfully and honestly as you can. No one will be judging you.

1. I frequently awaken during the night or I have a hard time falling asleep.
2. I sleep less than eight hours a night.
3. I am not rested when I wake up in the morning.
4. I am awake and refreshed only after one or more cups of coffee.
5. I am tired most or all of the time.
6. I have low stamina.
7. I get infections frequently.
8. I heal slowly from infections.
9. I often have bloating, gas, or indigestion.
10. I often experience constipation or diarrhea.
11. I frequently suffer from allergies, nasal congestion, chest congestion, or skin rashes.
12. I get headaches often.
13. I have back, shoulder, neck, or other muscle tension problems.
14. I have pain in my back, knees, hips, shoulders, or any other joint or joints.
15. Exercise makes me feel worse.
16. If I do not exercise, I feel worse.
17. I have little time for exercise, relaxation, or any real time for myself.
18. I have problems with my blood pressure.
19. I easily become short of breath or feel chest tightness or pressure.
20. My heart races often.

21. I easily get angry or irritated and lose my temper or get moody.
22. I often become irritated but keep it inside.
23. When I drink, eat, or smoke, I feel better.
24. I tend to worry a lot.
25. I often help others and rarely ask for help from others.
26. I often feel alone or lonely.
27. I get depressed.
28. I get anxious or often become highly emotional.
29. I am often tense and have a hard time relaxing.
30. My mind often races and I have difficulty being still.
31. I have difficulty becoming sexually aroused or maintaining arousal.
32. I cry at the drop of a hat.
33. I have difficulty making decisions.
34. I have trouble concentrating or remembering things.
35. I feel worse during the holidays or other family occasions.

Add up your score:

If your score is 106–140: Really out of control
If your score is 71–105: Somewhat out of control
If your score is 36–70: Slightly out of control
If your score is 35: You can write this book—you have good control over your Fear Response

As you proceed through this book, intermittently refer back to this questionnaire to see how you have made progress.

The goal of this questionnaire is not to make you feel bad but to show you to what degree your Fear Response has taken over your life. As you will see in the next chapter, recognizing your Fear Response is your first step to healing, achieving and regaining control of your balance.

2

FEAR

A Lack of Love

Detecting the Fear Response is not always easy. In fact, it is often like a game of Where's Waldo? You are unaware it exists until you know what to look for.

For most people, the Fear Response is so much the norm that you cannot remember life without it. You have forgotten what it is like to feel good, positive, and confident. You live long stretches of your life in your Fear Response without ever realizing it.

Then you finally get that vacation after months of ten-hour work-days. As soon as you're on the beach without a schedule, a cell phone, and fifty e-mails a day, your body begins to actually relax. You suddenly realize that you have been walking around with your shoulders up around your ears, your jaw imitating a vise, and your energy level pumped by excessive caffeine and energy bars. When you slow down a bit, escape your day-to-day routine, and enjoy enough downtime to appreciate the people and environment around you, it dawns on you: "I feel great! I wish I could feel like this every day."

Believe it or not, one of the major contributing factors to the great feeling you get while on vacation is that you breathe differently when your body is relaxed.

When in the Fear Response, most people breathe rapidly and shallowly or hold their breath altogether. That's right, you actually stop breathing many times throughout the day without even knowing it. Both of these breathing patterns reduce oxygen supply and signal the body to tense up.

When you are tense, you breathe improperly, using the chest cavity instead of the abdominal cavity, the area we normally associate with the stomach. Babies naturally breathe with their abdominal cavities. If you watch them, you can see their bellies moving up and down every time they breathe.

Abdominal breathing causes the stomach area to expand and rise with each deep breath. This pulls the diaphragm downward so that the space in the chest enlarges, allowing more air and oxygen to enter. With more air and oxygen in the chest, exhaling takes longer and the breathing rate slows down, which in turn slows heart rate, reduces blood pressure, and, at least briefly, turns off your Fear Response.

To feel the difference, try the following exercise, which I call the Balloon Breath, paying attention to how your body responds while you're doing it.

The Balloon Breath

Sit in a comfortable position.
Envision a deflated balloon located in the middle of your stomach.
Inhale slowly and deeply.
As you inhale, the balloon inflates, blowing up so that it gets big and round.
Notice that your stomach wall rises as you do this. (You may want to place a hand over your stomach to feel the sensation.)
Then exhale slowly and completely, letting the balloon deflate.
Notice that the abdomen falls down to normal.
Repeat for at least ten breaths.

If you concentrate on the balloon inflating and deflating, your inhalations and exhalations grow deeper, your breathing rate slows, and a feeling of calm takes over.

What did you feel like before this exercise? Physically? Emotionally? How do you feel now?

The point of this exercise is for you to feel—even if only briefly—

the difference in your higher energy level and mental clarity when the Fear Response is turned off. Don't worry. The length of time that you have this good feeling will expand as you learn the rest of the Love Response techniques throughout the book.

Most people are not attuned to how their bodies feel until they crash. For instance, most people do not think twice about walking until they blow a knee on the ski slopes or overdo it at the gym and find themselves on crutches.

The body and mind form a complex system that operates without a lot of conscious awareness or control on your part. This system contends with constant subtle challenges and automatically adjusts second by second throughout the day. If you are unaware of these challenges and how to resolve them, your system ends up working too hard, and the next thing you know you are ill.

However, if you learn to recognize when you are in the Fear Response, then the minute you notice that you feel bad, you can take action and stop small challenges from snowballing into full-blown problems. You can anticipate obstacles rather than slam into them unaware and ill-equipped. Your forward movement in life then progresses as if with the current of a river, in flow, aligned with your environment, not against it.

To stop the Fear Response, you not only need to recognize when it is active but also identify what set it off. That's the tricky part. Finding out why you are in the Fear Response can require some digging.

Imagine that you are white-water rafting with two friends. The rapids move fast, and you and one of your companions paddle hard to keep the raft afloat. The third friend, however, just jabbers on and drinks beer, happy to let you do all the work.

You try to focus on the course ahead, but you find yourself getting headachy—and increasingly irritated: "Look at him, going along for the ride while we are busting our butts. He always does this. He slacks off and then expects everyone else to . . ." Suddenly you realize that your raft is heading for a fallen tree. You jerk your oar back and steer clear of it. But the sudden motion causes the raft to lose balance and capsize.

How could you have avoided this situation?

You knew that your friend was unreliable, yet he upset and surprised you on the raft. You could have prepared yourself mentally for the behavior and then simply compensated for it. Or you could have let your friend know how you felt ahead of time and established some ground rules in advance of the trip. You would then have remained calm and in tune to the rhythm and flow of the river and its surroundings and stayed dry.

In this case, the challenge was not just the rapids or the fallen tree but your issue with this person. The root cause of your Fear Response was your inability to speak your mind, not only in this situation but also probably in the past as well.

TANGIBLE AND INTANGIBLE FEARS

You'd be surprised how many times people—including you!—live through the same stressful scenario over and over again without understanding the underlying cause of their misery. This occurs for one main reason: most of the challenges your system perceives as stress are unconscious. Stress to the body may be physical and tangible, such as the pain caused by cutting your finger. However, physical pain can also be intangible, caused by psychological, emotional, and spiritual stress. In the rafting example above, the tangible challenge was the fallen tree. The intangible challenge was your inability to express yourself.

Intangible challenges stress your body all the time without your knowledge. For instance, most of the time you are not aware when your blood sugar drops, because it is an intangible challenge. Your low blood sugar signals the body to respond to the brain with a feeling of hunger or weakness. The hunger is a tangible challenge, an uncomfortable sensation warning you that something is wrong with your body. The feeling of hunger prompts you to eat and return your body to a state of normal blood sugar.

Your body and mind use "feelings" or sensations such as hunger, neck or upper back tension, chills, fatigue, irritability, or frustration as a way of signaling that something is wrong in your internal or external environment. These feelings are the way your unconscious mind communicates with your conscious mind that its needs are not being met and action is required.

Most of the time, these feelings are relatively easy to identify and respond to. You're hungry, you eat. You're thirsty, you drink. You're tired, you rest. Other challenges, however, remain at the unconscious level and are not transmitted directly into conscious sensations. These challenges often go undetected for long periods of time because they are intangible, and that's what makes them so insidious.

Old silent memories can trigger plunges in blood sugar and drive your desire to eat even though you've just finished dinner. The unconscious belief that you are not safe (or finished with your work or ready for tomorrow's work or up to a challenge) can pump adrenaline through your body and mind, raise your blood pressure, increase your heart rate, and keep you awake. Feelings of shame often correlate with increased inflammation. It doesn't matter if the intangible challenge is physical, psychological, emotional, or even imagined. Whatever the threat, your brain searches to see if you have sufficient resources and asks these questions:

"AM I ENOUGH?"

and

"DO I HAVE ENOUGH?"

If the answer is "no," your brain perceives the situation as stress and the Fear Response kicks in, raising your blood pressure, quickening your breath, and pumping cortisol and adrenaline into your system in an attempt to ready your body to overcome the challenge.

THE FEAR RESPONSE AS A WARNING SYSTEM

Your body is equipped with a number of automatic and unconscious control systems that function without the need for thought and analysis.

For instance, when you stand up, the blood pressure in your brain falls as a result of the change in body position and gravity. An automatic physiological response rises to the occasion, quickening your heart rate and blood flow to the brain so that you do not pass out.

When you step outside into the cold without warm clothes on, your body shivers in an attempt to keep you warm. The shivering is automatic and unconscious, signaling to your conscious mind that it is too cold and you need your coat.

From breathing and blood flow to blinking and tear making to enzyme production and digestion to growing your hair, you perform the majority of your everyday actions on autopilot. You take climbing stairs for granted, but it is, in actuality, a very complicated task accomplished by a series of unconscious body systems—muscle groups, balance, flexibility, and several senses—working in unison. You don't think about what your body needs to do to climb steps. If you did, ascending one flight of stairs could take five minutes instead of twenty seconds. But if a ski accident were to put you on crutches, you would likely perceive climbing stairs as a challenge. Your brain would scan its resources, ask, "Am I enough? Do I have enough?" and find that the answer is "no." When the brain perceives it does not have the resources to handle a challenge, it calls upon the Fear Response to show up for duty.

Yes, your crutches can help you climb the stairs. Yes, an elevator is probably just a few feet away. But remember, these observations are the function of the logical mind. The rational side of the brain always shows up later, after your more primitive side has already turned on the Fear Response.

Your Experience Database

Most of the time, you can face a challenge with courage and confidence rather than apprehension because you believe you have the resources to handle it. These resources include everything that you have accumulated since the day you were conceived, such as your genetic information, immune system, muscle fibers, education, experiences, all bodily and mental abilities, and so on—everything that makes you who you are today. The past forms the basis of every thought in your head. All these accumulated experiences are stored in your mind's database and become files in your filing cabinet, allowing you to function efficiently in the present moment.

All it takes is one click on the right file in your filing cabinet, and you access all the information you need to complete a familiar task. To get dressed, you click on the file that tells you how to outfit yourself appropriately for the occasion or weather. The information stored in your filing cabinet is unique to you and your experiences and changes from day to day, moment to moment.

CONDITIONING, ASSUMPTIONS, AND PREDICTIONS

As infants, you possess virtually no data or files. What you do have, however, is an intact Fear Response. You are born on alert, highly sensitive and highly reactive.[1] You hear a loud sound, you cry. You discover that someone will come to help you and that this action results in a response that pleases you. This is the first file in your filing cabinet. Eventually, you learn that you will be fed and clothed. You learn how to communicate, crawl, walk, and run. You become educated and influenced by culture, religion, media, and the people around you. You learn about love, support, and comfort and to discern what is challenging from what is not. Your brain creates a reference list of positive versus negative experiences and automatic behaviors and actions associated with each. These are all stored in your filing cabinet based upon which your brain predicts your likely success or failure with a challenge.

Think about something that you have tried to do many times without success, such as skiing. The last time you tried it, you ended up on crutches. Now imagine that a potential romantic partner has suggested a skiing date. How do you feel about it? Confident or apprehensive? Most likely, since your past experience was negative, your brain will predict that the outcome will be negative again and stimulate your Fear Response simply in anticipation of falling on the slopes.

However, what if you decided to take skiing lessons, learned some skills, and gained some confidence? Your brain might predict a different outcome about skiing now that you have added fresh files to your filing cabinet and built up your resources. In general, the more resources your database contains, the less your Fear Response will run the show.

No matter how many resources you have, the first line of defense is paying attention to your Fear Response warning signals. As in the skiing example, these warning signals are not just physical. Very often, they take the form of negative emotions.

EMOTIONS

Your emotions exist to signal your body to act appropriately in given situations. Thus, emotions can have profound effects on your ability to cope with life challenges as you age.[2] Emotions significantly impact your ability to learn and store memory. In turn, your experiences, especially childhood experiences, significantly influence your emotions.

THE CHILDHOOD FACTOR

Research shows that early nurturing experiences help individuals handle challenges later in life and moderate the frequency and intensity of the Fear Response. For instance, animals that experience greater amounts of maternal licking and grooming have decreased behavioral signs of fearfulness in later life.[3] Nonnurturing early experiences, however, may accelerate the Fear Response and result in damaging health consequences.[4]

In humans, research demonstrates that intense, negative emotional experiences in early life can cause changes in the Fear Response that profoundly affect an individual's ability to cope with life challenges later in life. Studies also indicate that individuals brought up in "high-risk" families—families filled with neglect or abuse or lacking in nurturance and love—have a higher propensity for developing mental problems such as anxiety and depression[5] as well as physical health problems.[6]

NEGATIVE EMOTIONS, NEGATIVE MOOD, AND HEALTH

We know that negative emotions provoke the Fear Response. Dr. Candace Pert, for instance, believes that sadness produces biochemical changes that negatively affect every cell in the body so that every part of you is "sad"—from your hair follicles all the way down to your toes. Other research shows that undeniable links exist between depression or loneliness and the increased risk of heart disease,[7] diabetes,[8] and immune dysfunction;[9] between anxiety and a higher risk of heart disease and poor recovery from surgery;[10] between anger and hostility as risk factors for heart disease,[11] inflammation, and pain.[12] Increasingly, scientific evidence associates prolonged negative emotions and negative mood states with disease.

MARK: *Depressed and Lonely*

Mark, fifty-three, arrived in my office looking for inner peace. He complained of feeling depressed and anxious. He complained of rising blood pressure and daily problems with his stomach, including pain and heartburn. He had recently started on medications to treat each of the problems. He also complained of low energy and terrible sleep; he usually awakened in the middle of the night and was then unable to fall back to sleep. He often self-medicated with alcohol and more often than not awoke in the morning in a panic.

I asked Mark what had occurred recently that might be worsening his symptoms and behaviors. He answered that he had just gone through a divorce after being married for more than twenty years. He had two children and missed them terribly. He missed being part of the household. He missed having others to care for. The worst part, he told me, was that his children were acting resentful and angry toward him. He added that his marriage problems had started after his work went into decline. When his consulting business had begun to fail, his wife had lost interest in him and grown angry and resentful. He felt separate, like an outsider, from his family and the world. He felt that if anything were to happen to him, no one would care. "Why should they want to be around me?" he added. "I am miserable. I am lonely." The more alone he felt, the more depressed and anxious he became. The more negative his emotions, the worse he felt physically and the more he drank. The worse he felt, the more reclusive his behavior, exacerbating his loneliness.

EXERCISE

It's Your Turn to Notice How Negative Emotions Cause You to Feel

Close your eyes.

Think about something that angers or saddens you, then pay attention to the following sensations:

- What is happening with your breathing pattern?
- Notice if and where your muscles are getting tense.
- Notice other emotions or feelings that come up for you.
- Notice the thoughts that flow through your mind.

You may find that when you start thinking about something that upsets you, you cannot stop. You never seem to get resolution with your thoughts. Think about why this particular situation upsets you and if it reminds you of some other situation you may have experienced in your past. Pay attention as you go through your day. Is there a pattern to the way that you react?

QUESTIONS FOR YOU

- Are you aware of the negative thoughts that constantly run through your mind?
- Do you notice the negative emotions that trigger these negative thoughts?
- Do you know where the thoughts and emotions come from?
- Do you associate these negative emotions with an incident, experience, or person?
- Are you aware that every time you think bad about yourself, the Fear Response is set off?
- How do you see yourself? Positively or negatively?
- When you think about yourself, do you feel a positive emotion or a negative emotion?

How many of you wake up in the morning, look in the mirror and say, "Gosh, I love my thighs!" or "I am so incredibly beautiful!"? Most of you find faults or things you want to change when you look in the mirror. How many times a day do you beat yourself up for not doing something right or admonish yourself that you "should have" done this or that? Each time you behave this way, you activate the Fear Response. Your words imply that you are not good enough, that you are somehow bad, or that you need to be and do better.

It is likely that most of the time you put yourself down automatically and unconsciously. Your unconscious mind is so deeply programmed to see yourself in a negative light that it doesn't know anything different. When the information in your resource database points to a negative self-image, any situation that may challenge your self-esteem or self-confidence unconsciously will stimulate the Fear Response before your conscious mind registers what is going on.

FEELING GOOD ENOUGH

During your childhood, you began to define yourself, asking such questions as, "Am I loved?" "Am I smart?" "Am I capable of handling situations?" "Am I supported?" "Who am I with respect to my world?"

Most of you have learned to define yourselves through your external roles—as a wife or husband, doctor, janitor, Muslim, Christian, and so on. You have learned to solidify who you are by following the guidelines your culture or society set up for you. You have categorized and defined yourself through external means—by how much money you have, what school you attend, your job, your sexual preference, the shape of your body, marital status, and so on—all things that are subject to change. As you lose what you believe defines you, you feel lost and anxious. You realize you really don't know who you are. This translates to not feeling good enough and activates your Fear Response.

In contrast, the more confidence you possess in your knowledge of who you are, the more in control you feel. The more you feel supported and loved for who you are, the more capable you are in handling life's challenges and the less Fear Response you experience.

As a small child, you were likely full of energy. You loved to scream, run, investigate, and essentially get into everything—the closets, cupboards, garbage, toilet. Someone likely watched you constantly and invariably warned and admonished you for your actions, sometimes unnecessarily and harshly. Adults are often so stressed and frustrated that they scream, shout, or even hit their children in an effort to control them. The children then learn that it is not okay to explore and express themselves. This is how you learned shame, as well as the notion that the world is not a safe place. As you grew older, you learned from society, school, media, and culture the "appropriate" way to behave, look, and be, and this reinforced what you learned from your parents.

Some of you, unfortunately, had familial relationships that were abusive. As a result, you learned that you were not worthy and never safe, loved, or supported. The memory of abuse or neglect has stamped itself deeply into your mind and body. Every stress you experience stimulates that memory, especially when your identity is challenged.

Some of you, though, through family and friends, have learned that you are loved, that you are okay the way you are, and that you are supported, with or without external accomplishments. You have learned that you can maintain your balance despite situations that may challenge your external identity.

JANE: *Abandonment*

Jane was thirty-five years old at the time of her annual checkup. She complained of anxiety, irritable bowel, and inability to conceive for the past three years. She had been diagnosed with hyperthyroidism (overactive thyroid) four years before, when she had gone to the emergency room with a panic attack, palpitations, shortness of breath, and chest pain after discovering that her father had dropped dead from a heart attack. She took medication for her thyroid condition but still complained of ongoing anxiety. She worked sixty to eighty hours a week as an executive, exercised avidly, and described herself as a "perfectionist" in her work, in how she maintained her household, and her physical fitness. I could not find any abnormalities on her physical exam or in her blood work.

I asked Jane about her childhood. When she was four years old, living in Israel, her mother had left for the United States to start building a home for the family. Jane had stayed behind with her father, a very busy and successful businessman who spent most of his time working. She was not reunited with her mother for a year and a half. She remembered the feelings of loss at that time, how wonderful it was to reunite with her mother, and also how angry she was that her mother had left at all.

I asked Jane if she had ever sought therapy to work out her issues of loss and/or abandonment. She had not. In theory, the trauma of separation from her mother at a young age without sufficient support to enable her to cope effectively had led to a hyperactive Fear Response. The loss of her father, even though it had occurred much later in life, had re-created her childhood trauma of parental separation. Jane was not able to adapt to her father's death, and her Fear Response escalated out of control, resulting in panic attacks. The inability to conceive was also likely a by-product of her hyperreactive Fear Response, as well as her own issues around abandonment by her mother.

I explained to Jane that if she learned how to cope more effectively and work through her psychological distortions, she could possibly reverse her physiology, rid herself of her anxiety and irritable bowel, and perhaps conceive a child. I explained that though we could not change what had happened to her in her life, we could try to change how she had felt about herself at the time and how she coped, so that her brain might have a different frame of reference when it came to dealing with loss or being a mother. I recommended relaxation exercises and a cognitive behavioral therapist to address and change her distorted beliefs, thoughts, and feelings. I also suggested that she take up a form of exercise that would not send the message to her brain that she was in stress and running away from a lion.

Several months had passed when I received an e-mail from Jane. She had taken a leave from her job, gone into therapy, and enrolled in belly dancing and yoga classes. Not only that, she was now one month pregnant. A year later, she came to my office with a picture of her newborn daughter.

IT'S NEVER TOO LATE TO FIX IT

You can learn to control your Fear Response no matter what kind of family environment you grew up in. Very few of us had a perfect family. In fact, I don't know anyone who has, even those from so-called good families. Few of you had an "ideal" childhood, in which you received consistent and limitless love and support from your families and teachers; you were not exposed to negative influences from culture and media; and you did not experience financial uncertainty or threatening world events.

You can learn to live well and maintain balance. You can do this through outer resources such as advances in medicine, technology, and self-care behaviors and by developing your outer and inner resources, specifically the qualities of adaptability, flexibility, and resiliency. Then you will be able to face challenges with courage and the Fear Response will remain short-lived, as it should. The beauty of the Fear Response is that when life is in balance, it contains itself, so that its physiological changes remain beneficial and short-lived rather than harmful and protracted.

RESILIENCY AND ADAPTABILITY

Imagine an office full of people who are mostly the same gender and age. It is flu season, and half the office is out sick. Why doesn't the other half get sick? Why are at least half the people in the office going about their day, working, exercising, and, most important, not feeling miserable? What do they have that the sick folks do not?

They have sufficient resources in the form of strong immune systems. Their immune systems enable them to adapt to the sick environment and stay resilient against the virus.

Adaptability and resiliency allow you to maintain your balance and flow. Being "in flow" means moving smoothly with life's changes rather than resisting them; easily adapting and staying resilient despite the obstacles. Adaptability and resiliency are two essential qualities for staying out of the Fear Response.

Your ability to maintain resiliency depends on many factors, including genetic variability, nutrition, physical fitness, belief system, cultural influences, support system, environmental exposure, and life history, especially early life history. When these factors are positive, they contribute to your adaptability and resiliency in an additive way. When they are negative, they contribute to stress that accumulates over time. If stress outweighs your resources, the Fear Response takes over, and with it flexibility, adaptability, and resiliency diminish.

You can change the trajectory of your early life experiences and create a life that increases in adaptability and resiliency. You can grow more adaptable and resilient with age, rather than less so. You just have to know how.

EXERCISE

Feel the Love Response

Find yourself a comfortable position.
Close your eyes after reading this.
Imagine the face of someone you love.
See their face smiling at you.
Notice everything about them.
Notice how this makes you feel.
As you breathe in deeply and exhale completely, notice
    how you feel.

That feeling is a short burst of the Love Response as it turns off your Fear Response. As you proceed through the book, you will learn to turn off the Fear Response repeatedly and for meaningful lengths of time.

3

THE ANTIDOTE TO FEAR

The Love Response

STOPPING THE CYCLE

It is tantalizing to envision a life without fear and stress. But seriously, you would never get out of bed in the morning if you had nothing to work for or against or nothing pressing to do. You would be bored out of your mind.

You need the contrasting dynamics of stress and flow to move your life forward. You need stimulation. You need to know what you don't want in order to identify what you do want. You need the Fear Response to get off your butt and make things happen. The Fear Response becomes a problem only when it occurs for too long or too often. That's when it can destroy your life.

Your mission, if you should choose to accept it, is to control the Fear Response and use it only when necessary, keep it short, lessen your reactivity and defensiveness to life experiences, and spend the rest of your time living in joy and pleasure.

How? By activating the Love Response.

THE LOVE RESPONSE

The Love Response is a coordinated fusion of varied emotions, thoughts, positive neuropathways, and reward mechanisms that ultimately allow the body, mind, and spirit to maintain equilibrium even when faced with stress. It involves the release of hormones and peptides that reduce stress response activity, especially when negative emotions have caused the stress. The Love Response regulates the body's stress system, resulting in physical, mental, and emotional health and a life of balance.

By learning to activate the Love Response through practicing the techniques I will show you, you will be able to improve your self-confidence, sociability, and flexibility. You become a full participant in your own well-being and an advocate for your long-term health. You engage in the strategies that strengthen you and enable you to trust in your body's natural ability to heal itself. When you use the Love Response, you just might find that your visits to the doctor's office become rarer.

THE LOVE RESPONSE VERSUS THE FEAR RESPONSE

Although the Fear Response is beneficial, as it gets you out of harm's way and entices you to succeed in life, its associated behaviors, thoughts, actions, and attitudes are often negative and hurtful not only to you but also to others. For instance, a person who is drowning may reach out to grab on to the nearest object. That nearest object may be you, and subsequently you are pulled under the water and almost drown. Did this person intend to harm you? Probably not. He or she was just trying to stay alive. Fear drove those actions.

In contrast, love rarely, if ever, harms you or others. Actions generated from love tend to support and help, to engage and bring joy. Love's attitudes, beliefs, and emotions are positive and well intentioned. They do not evoke the Fear Response and its stressful physiological effects and are therefore healthier for you as well as those around you. Moreover, one action performed with the intention of love generates more love-based actions, almost automatically.

For instance, if someone lets you get in front of him or her in a long line, you are more prone to do the same. The opposite is also true. If someone cuts you off in traffic, you are more likely to be angry and cut someone else off. Actions generated from both love and fear tend to snowball, building momentum on one another until you find yourself proclaiming that you are having a bad day, bad week, month, year, or years. Instead, you can—in a few minutes and eventually seconds—change that momentum to a day, week, month, year, and years of joy and well-being.

Fear, Love, and Evolution

The Fear Response can rob you of your physical vitality and make you more inclined toward physical illnesses such as heart disease, diabetes, lowered immunity, and infertility, which reduce the chances of your survival and that of your offspring. For evolutionary purposes, this outcome is certainly not conducive to further propagation of the species![1]

In the state of love, however, you feel secure, safe, and supported. When you feel safe and supported, you are less likely to be hypervigilant, to be braced for a possible "lion," and more likely to relax, take your time, evaluate your available resources and tools, and actually use them to solve problems. With this greater confidence, you are more likely to attract more people and increase your available resources so that—evolutionarily speaking—you are a healthy, viable candidate with which to propagate the species.

How the Love Response Works: Hormones and Peptides

Love carries with it an ingrained biochemical function that creates bonding, attachment, and pleasurable sensations. Certain physical processes occur in the body and brain when you feel love and you give and receive affection. The collective result of these processes is the Love Response.

From a neurobiological perspective, it appears that certain circuits in the brain, along with the release of hormones and small proteins called peptides, influence your ability to love and bond. They influence the attachment created between parents and between parents and their infants. Love and affection (this includes loving touch) release these hormones and peptides. They, in turn, cause you to experience pleasurable sensations and positive emotions that enhance your desire to stay together and support each other.

The peptides and hormones released with love, including endorphins, oxytocin, dopamine, vasopressin, and nitric oxide, also perform another function: they help turn off the Fear Response, evoke the relaxation response, and create positive physiology.[2]

Endorphins, for instance, can create the sensation of euphoria and relief from pain. Dopamine opposes the effects of fear and improves your circulation and mood. Vasopressin and nitric oxide regulate your blood pressure and circulation, which are "off-regulated" with fear. In the Fear Response, the body usually produces adrenaline. In the Love Response, the body reduces the amount of adrenaline released.

BIOCHEMISTRY OF AFFECTION

Oxytocin serves many other functions with respect to the Love Response. It enhances social attachment and other social behaviors. Affection—loving touch in all its forms—is perhaps the most powerful trigger to release oxytocin in the body.

We see this clearly in maternal bonding.[3] When a mother nurtures her infant, her body produces oxytocin, thereby rewarding her for nurturing her infant and improving the child's chances of survival. For instance, a mother's touch can calm her baby. In fact, the mother is doing more than stopping her child from crying. Studies show that her body contact also stabilizes the newborn's body temperature, energy conservation, acid-base balance, and breathing rate. A mother's love and affection not only help the infant's stress system stay regulated but also her own system. The exchange of love and affection creates a positive loop that has positive affects on the giver and the receiver.[4]

Among adults, oxytocin contributes to the attachment between sexual partners. It is released during sexual intercourse so that you bond to your lover, making it more likely that you will choose each other again next time around. Both oxytocin and vasopressin are involved in the formation of social bonds and in promoting social recognition memory (i.e., you recognize the people you love). Both play a role in Fear Response regulation. Science, in fact, has repeatedly demonstrated that love and affection stimulate the release of hormones and peptides that improve mood, increase sociability, enhance attachment, and ultimately turn off the Fear Response.[5]

Even affection as simple as a hug releases oxytocin in both men and women. A University of North Carolina study showed that women have reduced blood pressure and cortisol after receiving hugs from their husbands.[6] Another study in a sample of 366 men and women investigated the relationship between brief warm social and physical contact among cohabiting couples as well as cardiovascular reactivity to stress. Individuals receiving partner contact had lower blood pressure and heart rate increases than did the no-contact group when exposed to stress.[7]

THE BIOCHEMISTRY OF LOVE: BRAIN CIRCUITS AND REWARD

Love induces a positive reward of peace, balance, and being in flow. Once you are rewarded positively, your memory registers this experience as pleasurable. The more positive experiences you accumulate in your memory, the more your unconscious mind predicts that all will be well in the future.

When you receive a reward for a job well done, you are more likely to repeat the action that brought about the positive outcome. New research links love to the brain's circuits that reinforce behaviors. These brain areas form a feedback loop so that every time you do something that produces a pleasant experience, the brain sends out signals to stimulate you to perform the same behavior again.[8] Hormones and peptides such as oxytocin and vasopressin control much of this feedback. For example: when you feel love, you may experience less physical pain as a result of the release of endorphins and morphinelike substances. These same chemicals can also improve your energy and cause you to experience a feeling of being high, the opposite of what you experience with perpetual fear.

THE BENEFITS OF BONDING

Ideally, bonding, attachment, and positive reward mechanisms persist throughout child development until a child has grown up to be a well-adapted, self-confident, social, and loving individual. In childhood, the brain is constantly growing and forming new nerve pathways in response to different environmental stimulants. The child's brain is very plastic, meaning it is highly influenced by changes in the environment and new information that is coming in. The brain is therefore constantly shifting, changing, and redirecting its nerve connections during the childhood period. The more positive rewards you experience as a child, the more input you impart into your brain and the more nerve pathways you create. This serves as the basis for you to be able to handle more experiences and to take in more information later. As you experience more positive rewards, the brain develops an increasingly better ability to take in new ideas, think clearly, and develop the capacity for abstract/intellectual thought.

The more a child incurs painful experiences, the more the memory of negative results sets into the brain and forms a negative loop. By the time the child becomes an adult, he or she will be more fearful or rageful when faced with a challenge and less likely to think clearly and rationally and solve problems.

This is why children who receive ample parental affection possess better adaptive behaviors and thereby benefit from less stimulation and shorter bouts of the Fear Response. No parent can give unconditional love to a child all of the time because parents peridocially experience stress and go into their Fear Response. But with more positive experiences such as nurturing, education, and love in early life, your emotional health is more likely to be sustained throughout your life.

Do your early childhood experiences seal your destiny? No. The Love Response allows you to change your early imprint—not by changing history but by changing your physiology.

BONDING AND PHYSICAL AFFECTION

Physical proximity and physical affection play an especially important role in bonding and its positive effects. It feels good to receive and give physical affection or touch. Such experiences stimulate the release of the peptides and hormones that produce a euphoric sensation or pleasant feeling and activate the brain reward center, encouraging you to do it again and again. Thus, the "bonding."

Interestingly, it appears that bonding is a process that occurs not only on the physical level through touch, but also on a cellular level. In his 1992 work *Evolution's End,* Joseph Chilton Pearce described how a cell from the heart forges connections with another: "If you isolate a cell from the heart, keep it alive, and examine it through a microscope, you will see it lose its synchronous rhythm and begin to fibrillate until it dies. If you put another isolated heart cell on that microscopic slide it will also fibrillate. If you move the two cells within a certain proximity, however, they synchronize and beat in unison." In other words, cells need other cells to survive, to live in harmony or balance. The heart cell's fibrillating when it is alone can be likened to our Fear Response activation. The cell's synchronizing when it is with other cells can be likened to the Love Response activation.

Bonding starts early for us. When mothers place their babies to their breast, their hearts are kept in proximity. The heart produces the hormone atrial natriuretic factor (ANF), which dramatically affects every major system of the body, including the central nervous system of the brain. As the mother holds the baby to her heart, the baby's heart rate synchronizes with her heart. "All evidence indicates that the mother's developed heart stimulates the newborn heart, thereby activating a dialogue between the infant's brain-mind and heart," says Pearce. "By holding her infant in the left-breast position with its corresponding heart contact, a major block of dormant intelligence is activated in the mother, causing precise shifts of brain function and permanent behavior changes."[9] In turn, Pearce says, the mother's contact with the infant causes permanent changes in her brain function, stimulating instinctive maternal behaviors.

Both infant and mother benefit from this beautiful dynamic.

HAPPIER IS HEALTHIER

Positive emotional states and positive thoughts, attitudes, and beliefs predict better health. Individuals who have a positive outlook show improved recovery after surviving acute medical events.[10] People who feel a strong psychological well-being tend toward lower cortisol levels, less inflammation, and better immune responses.[11] In general, happier individuals experience fewer Fear Responses.[12]

In my clinical practice, I have seen many times over the connection between positive thoughts, emotions, and attitudes and how good your body feels. The opposite is also true: the better your body feels, the happier you are.

 ELIZABETH: *Prayer*

Elizabeth was an eighty-year-old patient with complaints of depression and anxiety. She had a number of other medical problems, including heart disease, asthma, diabetes, and arthritis. She complained of depression and anxiety since her husband's death one year previously. She said she prayed every morning just to make it through the day.

My heart hurt, listening to her story, especially with these last words. I thought to myself, "If her words make me feel bad and my heart feels pain, what must they be doing to her, to her body, to her physiology?" I spoke with her about her morning prayer. I noted to her that the assumption behind her prayer was negative, a fear-based assumption that she was not going to make it through the day. I also explained that fear-based beliefs turned on the stress response, which worsened her physical and psychological symptoms. I asked her then, "Are you a fortune-teller? Do you know something that I don't know? Because I am the one with the M.D., and there is no scientific evidence supporting that you will not survive out the day."

She looked at me with a smile and shook her head, responding "No, I don't know these things. I am assuming, because my life is so hard." So I asked her if there was anything in her life that she was living for, anything that she appreciated. Her eyes and face lit up with joy as she spoke about her grandchildren. My heart too felt joyful and alive.

So I said, "Well, how about changing the words of your prayer? How about using words that reflect the truth, yet are positive and not stress provoking?" I told her that she didn't want to choose words that expressed expectations, because one really never knows what the day will bring. I asked her, "Pinch yourself, are you alive now?" Of course, the answer was a giggle and "Yes!" So I said, "How about this prayer: 'Thank you, God, for giving me life today.'" What a difference a sentence makes! She felt better simply by repeating the prayer. I knew she would be able to say it every morning from then on.

CHECK IT OUT!

Try this for yourself by noticing how you feel when you repeat each of the following two prayers.

- First repeat this prayer: "God, help me make it through the day."

  — Notice what you are doing with your breath: Are you breathing deeply or shallowly?
  — Notice how you are sitting: Are you sitting upright or are you hunched over?
  — Notice your chest: Does it feel open and light, or tense and heavy?
  — Notice the thoughts that arise: Are they pleasant or are they more stress provoking?

- Then repeat this prayer: "Thank you, God, for giving me life today."

- Notice again how your heart feels, as well as your body language and thoughts.

You may notice that as you say the first prayer, you feel a heaviness weighing you down. You may feel your shoulders collapsing forward and your chest caving in. When you say the second prayer, you may feel life and energy going up and down and through your body. You may feel like sitting up straight and tall and as though your breath is coming into your body more readily and smoothly. This is because your thoughts and beliefs, and the words with which you express them, affect your physiology and that of others too. Positive thoughts, beliefs, and words often can heal yourself and others.

THE LOVE PYRAMID

Love can help you heal. It is your cushion. The question is: How do you get on and stay on this path to wellness? By building your own personal Love Pyramid, which consists of:

- Social Love, the love you exchange with others
- Self-Love, the love and nurturance you give yourself
- Spiritual Love, the connection with Spirit or something larger than yourself and the altruistic works that flow from it

The Love Pyramid is a life structure that can help you override negative childhood conditioning and negative experiences from early life and keep your Fear Response in check until it's truly needed.

THE LOVE PYRAMID QUESTIONNAIRE

As a first step to building your Love Pyramid, fill out the following questionnaire.

Rate the following questions as follows:

Always true: 4
More often than not true: 3
Rarely true: 2
Not true: 1

Take your time in answering these questions as truthfully and honestly as you can. No one will be judging you.

1. I feel I am respected and supported by my romantic partner.
2. I feel I am respected and supported at work.
3. I can delegate responsibilities to others rather than do everything myself.
4. My personal relationships are more often calm, rather than tense and melodramatic.
5. My work relationships are more often calm and rational, rather than tense and stressful.
6. I feel that I can count on my friends or family to support me or to give me a shoulder to cry on.
7. I have adequate resources at work to turn to for complaining or expressing my needs.
8. I feel complete within myself, never needing to fill myself up with food or alcohol.
9. I value my own company and enjoy spending time alone.
10. I enjoy spending time doing things with other people.
11. I feel secure with myself.
12. I am good at making myself happy and giving myself the things I need.
13. I often treat myself to "I love myself" gifts.
14. I often treat others with "I love you" gifts.
15. I am honest and loving with myself about my faults and imperfections.
16. I am honest and loving with others about their faults and imperfections.
17. I am able to be intimate without feelings of shame or guilt.
18. I am good at problem solving.
19. My coworkers would describe me as being good at problem solving.
20. I do not cast blame on myself when something goes wrong.
21. Nor do I cast blame on others.
22. I can take criticism without falling apart.
23. I can offer criticism with compassion and without being hurtful.
24. I can listen without interjecting or thinking up my answer before the other person is finished.

25. I have a spiritual belief system and/or feel connected to nature, God, or Spirit.
26. I often take walks or engage in activities out in nature.
27. I often volunteer my time or efforts to help others.
28. I feel that I belong to some kind of community, one made up of friends or other people who share my interests, such as a spiritual or religious belief system or love of a sport or hobby.
29. I have a hobby.
30. I eat healthful and exercise my body.
31. I feel that I have a life purpose.
32. I giggle or laugh often.
33. I can trip and fall flat on my face without feeling too embarrassed or bad about myself.
34. I can laugh at myself.
35. I think I am perfect just as I am, imperfections and all.

Add up your score:

If your score is 140: You should be writing this book.
If your score is 106–139: You could use a little light reading of this book.
If your score is 71–105: You might want to take careful notes.
If your score is 35–70: You might want to read this book a few times over.

You can use this questionnaire to help you understand which part of the Love Pyramid most needs attention: Social Love, Self-Love, or Spiritual Love. Like the Fear Questionnaire, these questions are not meant to make you feel bad or guilty. Rather, this exercise prepares you for the all-important first step in your healing process: becoming aware of what is going well in your life and what still needs work.

4

THE SHIELD

Your Tool for Transformation

You are about to walk into your boss's office and ask for a raise. Your heart races. Your voice trembles. Your hands are clammy. You need to build a case for yourself, yet you can barely remember your middle name at the moment, much less all your contributions to the company that merit a salary increase. In short, your Fear Response has taken over.

How can you regain your composure so that you do not appear like a blithering idiot?

You use your SHIELD, a simple technique that instantly fends off your Fear Response and returns you to a state of calm, even in the heat of the moment.

The advantage of the SHIELD is that you can use it anytime you need it, even in the middle of a pressured situation. Easy and practical, this technique changes your energy from stressful to calm, negative to positive, from fear to love, in just seconds.

The SHIELD heightens your awareness so that you can home in on the sources of your Fear Response. It also helps you switch off the Fear Response and initiate the Love Response. It restores positive physiology, so that your health, well-being, and life circumstances benefit.

How I Discovered the SHIELD

Spiritual leaders know at the core of their being that they are not alone, that they are loved and protected. Of course, many of them also have hundreds of people surrounding them who care for their day-to-day survival needs and, in effect, *shield* them from the commotion of everyday life.

Everyone deserves a shield. I came to this realization one Friday afternoon while driving in rush-hour traffic. It seemed as though every few minutes, someone cut me off. As I sat behind the wheel, fuming with frustration, and screaming a few choice words at the rude drivers, I noticed the familiar feeling of guilt creep up. I thought to myself: "How could you react in such a way! You are a spiritual teacher. How could you curse like this?" I continued to berate myself: "The Dalai Lama would never behave this way!" With this thought, I laughed. The Dalai Lama likely would not behave this way because *he would not be driving. He would have a driver.*

This realization made it clear to me that everyone should have a shield—maybe not in the form of an entourage of people who handle all the stressful tasks of life, but a spiritual shield that can help you quickly shift out of stress and fear and stay in joy and love more often.

The SHIELD Mnemonic

The SHIELD serves both as a calming visualization as well as a mnemonic (a memory device), so in times of overwhelming stress, you can easily remember the steps of the process.

The following is the SHIELD in a nutshell. I will give you detailed instructions in a little bit. For now, know that each letter of the SHIELD stands for the actions you are to follow:

S   *Slow down* and visualize the white or golden light enveloping you in love and protection.
H   *Honor* what you feel or experience. Avoid judging your feelings as bad or wrong. Just acknowledge them.
I   *Inhale*
E   and don't forget to *Exhale*
L   *Listen* to your thoughts, feelings, and sensations. Ask: How

am I being reminded that I am not enough or do not have
enough? Listen to the answer.

D **Decide** to heal and shift out of the Fear Response and into the
Love Response.

When to Use Your SHIELD

Use your SHIELD anytime you become aware of your Fear Response.

At this point, you still may not be able to tell when you are in
your Fear Response. So how do you know when to use your SHIELD?
Start out with the most obvious situations: anytime you feel like
screaming at someone or if you are tired, irritable, or in pain for any
reason, use your SHIELD.

Benefits of the SHIELD

The more you use the SHIELD, the more aware of your Fear Response you will become. In fact, the main objective of the SHIELD is
to help you develop awareness, to learn how to tune in to what and
how you feel, physically and emotionally. The SHIELD enables you to
achieve the very first step of the healing process: awareness that you
are in the Fear Response.

As you get better at using the SHIELD, it becomes a primary
method for getting you out of the Fear Response and into the Love
Response.

If, in the beginning, you manage only the awareness part of the
SHIELD, congratulate yourself. Being aware of when you are in the
Fear Response is a great accomplishment. However, as you practice
all the steps of the SHIELD whenever possible, eventually your
awareness of the Fear Response will become second nature and you
will learn how to shift into the Love Response whenever necessary.
The main thing to keep in mind is that anytime you practice *any* of the
steps of the SHIELD, you begin to deactivate the Fear Response and
start your shift into the Love Response.

About Awareness

Since your reactions are mostly unconscious and automatic, they usually occur long before your conscious mind even registers a situation.

That is why you can be in your Fear Response without actually knowing it. You may think you are "in balance" but are simply oblivious that you are not. Remember, balance does not refer to "being still," because nothing in life is static. Balance refers to being still within yourself so you can be attentive to subtle changes and adapt to them gracefully.

WHY AWARENESS IS NECESSARY

When you are still inside, you can hear, see, sense, and smell. You can be *aware*. You can be alert in the way animals can detect danger before they see it or the way early Native Americans knew it would rain long before a drop fell. Awareness sharpens your perceptions of what is happening around you and within you, physically and emotionally, so that you can respond appropriately.

AWARENESS EXERCISE

Read this exercise and then practice it before going on.

> Close your eyes.
> Concentrate on the base of your spine or the lower part of your back. How does it feel—tight, relaxed, achy?
> Imagine sitting in your favorite place, indoors or outdoors, surrounded by plenty of food, money, friends, and loved ones.
> Notice how your lower back or spine feels.
> Now imagine the opposite: you are destitute, with little food, money, or personal support.
> Have the sensations in your lower back or spine changed?

The awareness you have just experienced is only the beginning. As you practice the SHIELD, you will begin to sensitize yourself and thereby gain access to the deepest recesses of your mind and heart.

USING YOUR SHIELD

Let's slowly go over the steps of using the SHIELD visualization and mnemonic.

You are angry, in pain, or frustrated. You are in your Fear Response. What do you do?

Say the word "SHIELD" as you . . .

Slow down

Take a moment to visualize your SHIELD. Slow down and imagine a golden sun above your head. Imagine the sun's divine rays shining down on you, filling up every part of your body, starting with the head, the neck, shoulders, and arms, then the torso, legs, and feet. See this golden light spreading out, encircling you, forming a SHIELD of white light. Within this SHIELD are those who love you. For instance, imagine that your favorite grandmother is part of this light, embracing you in her arms. This is your SHIELD of love, comfort, and protection. Once you start to visualize your SHIELD, you begin to deactivate your Fear Response.

The more often you build your SHIELD, the stronger it will get. If you have problems fully visualizing the ball or rays of light or your loved ones standing near you, these images will fill themselves in as you practice.

If you are having difficulty imagining your SHIELD of light, or for a deeper experience, go to www.audible.com/loveresponse to listen to a complimentary audio download of *The Love Response* meditation and exercise. Track 1 will help you visualize your SHIELD.

Honor yourself

Would you blame a hurt baby for crying? Probably not. Just as you would hold and comfort a crying baby, do so for yourself. When you have negative feelings, just acknowledge them, without judgment, no matter how irrational or infantile they seem. These feelings are "leftovers" from your child self and its negative memories. Together, they trigger your Fear Response. The Fear Response is the only way your infant side knows how to express itself: Basically, it is screaming "Something hurts. I don't know what exactly. It just hurts. Fix it!"

When your Fear Response is inappropriate, when your feelings of anger, fear, shame, or other negative reactions are out of proportion to the situation at hand, much like a child's, you know that something or someone has jabbed at a hidden wound. This is your opportunity to heal that wound.

ABOUT HIDDEN WOUNDS

Consider this: You are driving. Your friend in the passenger seat taps your shoulder to get your attention and show you something interesting. You tell your friend to let you drive and that you will look later.

Now, what if you had a big, gaping, oozing sore on your shoulder? Your friend does the exact same thing as in the previous scenario, but this time you have a preexisting wound. How would you react to this tap on your shoulder? You might scream! You might be very upset. How could your friend be so insensitive? How dare your friend not pay attention to your needs? You might overreact to your friend because you have a preexisting wound. The tap on the shoulder is no longer simply a distraction. It now hurts.

Everyone has wounds. Everyone has suffered negative experiences that live deep within the memory. Throughout life, stressful events stir these memories, poking at the wounds and causing you to automatically react with fear, anger, shame, or other negative emotions. Consciously, you may have forgotten about these wounds—or told yourself they no longer matter. What remains, however, is the belief or assumption that resulted from the experience. For instance, a bully in third grade used to call you "stupid." Although it happened long ago and you have since graduated from an Ivy League school, you still carry the unconscious belief that you are not smart enough. Now anytime someone challenges your aptitude, you react automatically, with defensiveness or anger. At the same time, an automatic physical action accompanies that emotion. When you feel shame, you eat. When you feel anger, you lash out indiscriminately.

If you feel irritable, frustrated, tired, in pain, cranky, or whatever, do not chastise yourself. Just observe and become aware of and honor your wounds, knowing that there is always a reason your body is in the Fear Response.

How do you know you are in the Fear Response?

When you feel bad, you are in the Fear Response. It is that simple.

Yet, in a world where frustration and pressure are the norm, even identifying when you feel good or bad can take a little practice. It helps if you can view your life from a distance, as if you are a silent witness to what occurs inside you and around you. You can learn to be a silent witness in several ways. One of the easiest is through exercises that increase awareness.

PRACTICING AWARENESS

Awareness hones your skills of listening and paying attention to your everyday existence.

Awareness involves being able to take in the present instant, as if you are looking at your environment through a wide-angle lens, able to take in the entire field.

When you are first learning awareness, practice on simple, everyday tasks.

PRACTICE AWARENESS WHILE YOU . . .

- **Take a shower:** Appreciate the aromas of the soap and shampoo, the feel of the lather, the sound of the water, the sensation of the shower spray on your skin.
- **Walk:** Appreciate the color of the sky and flowers, the rustle of leaves in the wind, the sound of a car as it zooms by.
- **Eat:** Savor the colors on your plate, the food's texture and tastes.
- **Listen:** Tune in to the sound of a person's voice. Discern not only his or her words but the emotions expressed behind the words.
- **Speak:** Tune in to your own voice. What words are you using? What is the message behind your words? What are you feeling as you speak?
- **Breathe:** Observe the sensations in your body when you breathe or stretch.

AWARENESS EXERCISE: OBSERVING WHAT YOU EAT

Get yourself a morsel of food, such as a piece of chocolate, raisin, tomato, carrot, or some other food.

Look at what you have chosen. Study it as if you are viewing
  it through a camera lens. What do you see?
Bring it to your nose. What do you smell?
Close your eyes and cup it in your hands. What do you feel?
Put it in your mouth. What do you taste? What is its
  texture? What is the taste or the experience of chewing
  this food?
How does it feel as it goes down your throat?
What, if any, thoughts or emotions are coming up for you?

Awareness Exercise: Observing Your Body and Your Emotions

Focus on the sensations in your body as you say the words listed
below. Do this exercise with someone else, or simply repeat each of
these words out loud, one at a time. As you say the word, pay attention to what you feel. Notice, for instance:

- How your chest feels
- What happens with your breath—is it shallower or deeper?
- Any tightness or ache in your chest
- If you have any emotions or feelings associated with the word
- If you feel good or bad with each of these words

Do not rush this exercise. Give yourself time to identify your feelings and bodily sensations around each word or phrase.

Sad
Joyful
Not enough time
Plenty of time
Open
Closed
You are bad
You are good
White sandy beach
Garbage dump
Injustice

Triumph
The face of someone who angers you or someone you dislike
The face of someone you love

I cannot tell you how many times patients come to my office complaining of one thing and leave my office understanding that their complaint was not the real issue. As I walk them through the exercises of awareness, they learn nonjudgment. They learn to tune in to their Fear Response and begin the process of uprooting its real cause.

Here is an example of how I used an awareness exercise to get at deeper issues with my patient Lilly.

 LILLY: *Case History*

Lilly was a forty-five-year-old woman with chronic neck and back pain that had gotten worse over the past few months. She complained of poor sleep, fatigue, depression, and anxiety, which all worsened with stress. She also complained of her medications not working.

Lilly was indeed under a lot of stress. Being out of work, she was worried about her finances. The thought of needing to leave her home and move into a smaller place upset her. She felt like a complete failure. She comforted herself with fatty foods but ended up feeling worse. She gained weight, felt unattractive, and worried she would never date again. She felt very alone.

Lilly's childhood had been very difficult. Her father had died when she was an infant, and her mother, an alcoholic, had never remarried. Her mother was neglectful and verbally abusive. Lilly's older sister rebelled against their mother, leaving Lilly to "keep the' house." As a child, Lilly thought that if she kept quiet, behaved, and did what she was told, perhaps her mother and sister would be nicer to and less angry at her.

Lilly never received the support and love she needed from her mother or father. She did not feel secure as a child or as an adult. Therefore, any loss of what she thought was her support structure caused her to feel imbalanced or stressed and aggravated her physical problems. Anytime she felt deprived, she would feel empty and lonely, hungry for love and attention. To fill this void, she turned to food, which was temporarily soothing.

I led Lilly through an exercise that could help her see the source of her problem. I asked her to focus on her back pain. She described it as a stiffness that was moving up her lower back; two hot spots at the base were the most painful. She reported that it felt like a tight muscle that made her hold herself stiffly. The rest of the session proceeded in this way:

ME: Can you see if there is something causing the tight feeling in your back?

LILLY: I see a gray rubber band that is hard and taut.

ME: Can you see yourself inside this rubber band? If so, what does it feel like?

LILLY: Yes, I can get inside the rubber band. It is hard to breathe. It feels like a panic attack.

ME: Can you follow the rubber band to its source?

LILLY: It is coming from the very base of my spine.

ME: Can you cut the rubber band?

LILLY: Yes. Wow! I feel such relief.

ME: Can you place yourself or your awareness into the space that has been created by cutting the rubber band?

LILLY: Yes, I can. Wow. I feel peace and safety. I see the color purple everywhere.

ME: Now try to stay in this space, breathe into it, until it feels like it's becoming larger.

LILLY: It feels exhilarating. There is only one hot spot left now. It will not budge.

ME: Can you move your awareness into this hot spot?

LILLY: Yes. I feel a squeezing sensation, a feeling of anxiety and shortness of breath. It feels like a small fist. I am seeing a vision of my childhood. I am afraid. I see my mother. She is making me go down to the basement. I don't want to go. I am scared of the mice and rats down there.

It was now clear to Lilly, as it had long been evident to me, that she had difficulty trusting, and much of this was related to her relationship with her mother. Lilly could now be given tools to heal this distrust.

Our dialogue continued.

ME: Lilly, you are loved and supported. If there are mice or rats in the basement, they will not hurt you. You are safe and protected. Please repeat these words to yourself: "I trust that I am supported and loved." Now breathe into the base of your spine as you continue repeating the words "I trust that I am supported and loved." And when you are ready, tell me what you feel.

LILLY: I feel a sensation of lightness and relaxation. I am having a hard time holding on to it. I am beginning to feel unsteady. I can feel the anxiety seeping through.

At this stage, I felt that Lilly might feel safer if she opened her awareness to some "higher" or divine influence.

ME: Lilly, I invite you to direct your awareness to the crown of your head and to imagine a beautiful light coming from the sun above, coming through your crown. Continue repeating the words "I trust that I am supported and loved."

LILLY: My head feels like it is full of light. I feel calmer. It feels like the same open safe space that I found in my back earlier.

ME: Try breathing into this space. You are safe and loved. Now bring this feeling and this light down the base of your spine. Imagine that the light is extending down through from the base of your spine deep into the earth, past the rocks, past the water, and deep into the center of Mother Earth. Once there, you can retrieve more support and nurturance from Mother Earth. Then bring that support and nurturance back up to the base of your spine.

LILLY: I feel calm and relaxed. I feel grounded. The feeling is staying with me.

ME: Now bring the light up to your chest, to your heart, breathe into your chest, breathe into your heart, and repeat your positive verbal command "I trust that I am supported and loved." Repeat this ten times. When you are done, let the light and your breath spread throughout your entire body, repeating your positive verbal command as often as you wish.

I instructed Lilly to do this guided imagery exercise every day for at least a month. On her next visit, Lilly told me she was sleeping better and her body aches had ceased. She also had a date that night!

WHAT CAN YOU LEARN FROM LILLY'S EXPERIENCE?

When I guided Lilly through an exercise of awareness, she used her physical complaints as a map to their buried emotional roots. Her physical pain guided her to her hidden wounds. By creating a safe environment in my presence and by using the SHIELD imagery on her own, Lilly could become still enough to listen, reflect, and heal.

INHALE
and
EXHALE

What happens to a baby's breathing as the infant cries? I remember my niece used to cry so hard sometimes, I worried she was cutting off the oxygen supply to her brain! But when I picked her up and cradled her in my arms, her crying tapered off, and she automatically began taking long, deep breaths, as if she were sighing. Once she felt safe and comforted, she began to breathe normally again.

Big lesson here: You cannot turn off the Fear Response if you are not breathing! Take a moment. Are you breathing correctly?

I find when I tell myself to just "breathe," I freeze, which defeats the whole purpose. But if I instruct myself to just concentrate on the inhale and then concentrate on the exhale as distinctive events, my breathing grows deeper and steadier almost immediately.

TRY IT YOURSELF

Inhale deeply, until there's no more room in your chest for
   more air.
Exhale completely, until all the air is expelled from your
   lungs.
Repeat ten times.
When you repeatedly inhale and exhale this way, you quiet
   the mind and body and bring about a state of calm and
   peace.
If you find yourself overwhelmed, anxious, or upset, try this:

- Close your eyes or keep them open.
- Inhale, and don't forget to exhale.
- Observe your breath as it enters and leaves, as you inhale and exhale.
- Count down to yourself from 10 to 1 with each breath. Or repeat a word or a phrase such as "Peace and calm" or "In peace, out tension." Or hold an image in your mind, such as

the smile of someone you love or being held by someone who loves you.

- Imagine your SHIELD of light shining upon you, comforting and warming you.
- When you are done, examine how you feel.

Repeat this technique several times until you feel better. You can do this anywhere, anytime, under any circumstances. It can only help you.

LISTEN

Now that you are quiet inside, you can look past your Fear Response and find the hidden wound that triggered it. To find the wound, ask yourself what I call the Big Four questions below and *listen* to the answers. As you do this, keep in mind that no one and no situation "makes you feel bad." You already feel bad, and the person or situation is just reminding you of that.

THE BIG FOUR QUESTIONS

Ask yourself:

- Why am I reacting this way?
- What wound from my past is this current situation reopening?
- Why do I feel bad in this situation?
- In what way is this situation reminding me that I feel that I am not enough or do not have enough?

The answers to these questions usually involve not feeling good enough for one reason or another. Some aspect of the circumstance you are in leaves you feeling disrespected or taken for granted and unimportant. I have found that there is no need for a lot of self-analysis or dialogue here. It always comes down to those same questions and the answers you find.

Do not feel bad if you do not find the answers right away. As you practice and learn more techniques and tools throughout this book, it will become easier. The answer to your question can be simple: you need to feel more loved and supported. As a remedy, you can implement the visualization you just learned—allowing yourself to be enveloped by your shield of divine light as you breathe in the love of the earth—while repeating the positive verbal command "I trust that I am loved and supported."

OLD MEMORIES RESURFACE

I recall being out for a night on the town with girlfriends from work many years ago. I was dressed to the nines, high heels, makeup, the works. A man, whom I did not find attractive or interesting, talked to everyone at the table except me. I knew I was attractive and smart. And I knew I did not find this man even remotely appealing. Still, I felt hurt that he ignored me. This made no sense to me.

I went through the steps of the SHIELD. I slowed down and envisioned my shield of white light. I honored my anger and insecurity, inhaled and exhaled, then asked myself "Why do I feel bad? In what way is this situation reminding me that I feel that I am not enough or do not have enough? What wound from my past is this current situation reopening?"

I quickly saw a vision of myself as a teen, feeling overweight, ugly, and ignored by the boys in school. I now had a great figure and attracted a lot of men. Yet no matter how much male attention I received, I still possessed this insecurity deep in my unconscious. I was still that ugly girl in high school. Deep down, I felt that I was still not enough.

By doing the steps of the SHIELD, I discovered an unconscious negative belief about myself, a belief that had long ago lost its relevance to my life. As a remedy, I envisioned my teen self surrounded by the shield of unconditional love and light. I comforted her in my arms and told her how beautiful and magnificent she was. I imagined both of us were repeating these words: "I am loved and lovable and perfect just as I am." The more I practiced this imagery, the less the insecurity reared its dreadful head.

The SHIELD enables you to identify your negative beliefs hiding in your deep recesses and lay them out front and center. Once you do this, you can consciously and actively change them through the SHIELD's final step.

DECIDE

Once you've become aware of a hidden wound, you can **decide:** Will you stay in your Fear Response, reliving over and over again the pattern around your old wound and unconscious negative belief? Or will you do what it takes to heal yourself and shift into the Love Response?

If you choose the latter, you choose to change your physiology and your life. You choose to replace your negative belief with a positive one. I call this your Active Belief System.

Your Active Belief System is a positive set of thoughts and assumptions about yourself and your life that you consciously and deliberately create. You build your Active Belief System by reprogramming your unconscious mind. You implant a new belief that begins as a small seed and eventually grows, uprooting and replacing the old belief until it is no longer there. Without replacing your deep negative beliefs, it is difficult to stay positive either emotionally or in your physiology. If, however, you change your beliefs and attitudes from passive negative beliefs to a positive Active Belief System, your physiology will follow suit.

POSITIVE VERBAL COMMANDS

The most basic components of your Active Belief System are positive verbal commands. Positive verbal commands are reprogramming tools that influence your memory to create good habits and beliefs, while overriding the negative ones that have accumulated over time. Remember: the unconscious mind does not have a will of its own; it only holds beliefs based on your lifetime of experiences. If you repeat a new belief to the unconscious mind enough times, it will eventually treat it as fact.

It isn't enough just to repeat the positive verbal command, as you would with an affirmation. Positive verbal commands take place within the context of practicing the SHIELD. When you combine verbal commands with positive physiology, you no longer have only words but a positive *experience* that your mind and body can assimilate into a new set of positive behaviors.

You remember experiences better than you remember words. The unconscious mind works the same way. It is more likely to believe the experience of being loved rather than the words that you are loved, especially when the experience recurs frequently. By using your SHIELD to reinforce positive verbal commands, the experience of being loved becomes part of your new internal programming.

In the beginning, you do not even need to believe the words you say to yourself. In fact, if you find yourself resisting the command, you know that you have hit the mark! If you are resisting the words, it means you have come upon an old wound or "leftover" within you that wants to stay buried. It is resisting the change. For this reason, it is even more important for you to get at it and continue your efforts.

The aim of repeating positive verbal commands is to override the negative belief that currently exists in your mind, so that eventually you react, think, behave, and feel differently. Positive verbal commands work because they are directed at your deep unconscious beliefs while you are in the positive physiology elicited through the SHIELD or, in fact, any practice or activity that puts you in the relaxation response.

For instance, you can get into the relaxation response by using verbal commands as your repetitive focus or "mantra" as you breathe in and out. Inhale: "I trust I am loved and supported"; exhale: "I trust I am loved and supported." If you practice a form of mediation, such as tai chi, yoga, transcendental meditation, or mindfulness, you can insert the positive verbal command into the last few minutes of your meditation.

I HAD TO LOVE MYSELF

Remember I told you that I started healing myself by saying, "I love myself"? I didn't know it then, but this was the beginning of my own Active Belief System. Initially, I constantly argued with myself about it:

Positive verbal command: I love myself
Subconscious: No, you don't.
Positive verbal command: Yes, I do. I love myself.
Subconscious: No, actually you don't.
Positive verbal command: YES, I DO, I LOVE MYSELF! I LOVE MYSELF!

So it went on and on, back and forth. But over time, the negative, subconscious voice diminished in volume, not so sure of itself.

Rarely, now, it shows up as an audible squeak, but never as the all-knowing, controlling voice of my past.

I also found that when I repeated the command, I felt calmer, less anxious. I felt my physiology changing, growing more relaxed and positive. Over time, I began reacting differently to how people behaved toward me, which, of course, changed the way others responded to me.

THE LOVE RESPONSE FOR USING POSITIVE VERBAL COMMANDS

Use positive verbal commands when you feel . . .
- Depressed
- Anxious
- Overwhelmed
- Angry
- Guilty
- Ashamed
- Distracted
- Bad about yourself or about someone else

Use positive verbal commands anytime at all—even when you feel good.

How to put your positive verbal command into action
- First, choose a positive verbal command. A good one to start with is "I am enough, I have enough." (I will suggest a variety of commands that you can use in different situations as you read along in the book.)
- Repeat this command as often as possible, even while brushing your teeth, falling asleep, or driving the car.
- When you first repeat the positive verbal command, do so during or after a self-nurturing, loving, or positive experience. For instance, do this just after meditation, after a fun lunch day with a friend or a great day of shopping, after playing with your pet or hanging out with loved ones, or even after a funny movie. When you do this, the mind and body associate the positive verbal command with the positive experience. So when you repeat the command later during your day, the words will evoke your earlier positive feelings.

EFFECTIVE REPROGRAMMING THROUGH THE RELAXATION RESPONSE

The SHIELD is most effective when you elicit the Love Response on a regular basis. You can do so by visualizing your Shield and inhaling and exhaling with a focus for an extended period of time, perhaps ten to twenty minutes. Or you can quiet the mind and body in a different meditation method that works for you. If you implement loving and healing imagery during your relaxation, you further activate the Love Response.

In the last few minutes of the relaxation, repeat your positive verbal command. Then repeat the command throughout your day. The command cues your body to relax, which in turn stimulates positive physiology.

Being a busy person myself, I know it is difficult to find twenty minutes a day for meditation. So I am not asking you to. If you have a meditation practice and this is easy for you, wonderful. Otherwise, I simply encourage you to do the SHIELD, even if it is only two to three minutes at a time. Do as much as you can and increase the time slowly. There is no right or wrong here, just what feels right for you. I find music or guided relaxations on audio extremely helpful, as it is often easier to quiet the mind while listening to a soothing voice and beautiful music. Go to www.audible.com/loveresponse for a complimentary audio download of *The Love Response* meditations and exercises. Tracks 2 and 3 are two of my favorite guided meditations. Start with these and expand your relaxation library as you see fit.

RELAXATION BUDDIES

Many of my patients find that it is easier to meditate with other people. Changing old behaviors and thoughts does not happen overnight. It is a lifelong process, so it is important to allow others to help you. You can work with a therapist, join a meditation group, or get a pet if that is practical. You can practice yoga with another person, listen to a relaxation CD, or walk with awareness in nature. All of these experiences can help you recognize your Fear Response more quickly and implement your SHIELD more effectively.

The SHIELD in Use

I personally use the SHIELD in my daily life and know that the method works. Not too long ago, I had an argument with my sister. We are very close, but we have had our share of sibling rivalry and fights. The argument itself was silly, but my sister stormed out of the room and I was left seething and angry. The only thing going through my mind was "What's her problem?" I had the choice of staying that way, but I instead chose to do my SHIELD. I surrounded myself with unconditional love and light. I began inhaling and exhaling and honoring the way I felt. As I became quieter, I found that the argument brought back feelings of guilt and shame that I had had as a child—guilt for taking attention away from my older sister. I knew that I had to feed myself compassion. I began repeating my positive verbal command "I am loved and perfect just as I am." Within minutes, my anger dissipated. My negative thoughts turned to compassionate ones. After filling myself with compassion, I opened my eyes and extended this compassion to my sister. Just as I did this, my sister walked through the door, apologizing for getting so angry. I apologized too, and we were able to resolve the argument without resorting to any more harsh words or feelings.

THE SHIELD CHEAT SHEET

SLOW DOWN and visualize your shield of loving, healing white light.

HONOR your feelings, experiences, emotions, attitudes, and behaviors without judgment. Just observe your feelings as if you were a silent witness. Remember that they are pointing you to hidden wounds.

INHALE, and don't forget to EXHALE. This will deactivate the Fear Response and shift your physiology so that you can become quiet enough to understand the root cause of your Fear Response.

LISTEN to your thoughts, emotions, and the sensations in your body as you ask the Big Four questions:

- Why am I reacting this way?
- What wound from my past is this current situation reopening?
- Why do I feel bad in this situation?
- In what way is this situation reminding me that I feel that I am not enough or do not have enough?

Listen to the answers and what your unconscious mind is trying to tell you.

DECIDE to heal yourself and change your physiology. Use Positive Verbal Commands to override your negative beliefs and substitute your Active Belief System in its place.

PRACTICE, PRACTICE

I strongly recommend that you practice your SHIELD as often as possible. When in doubt, use your SHIELD. The more you practice the SHIELD, the more the reprogramming takes hold. Do the SHIELD at home, in your office, or in your car, during any everyday activity. Do it anytime you feel bad or challenged. In a few days, you will begin to notice how you behave differently in stressful situations and feel much better in general. The more my patients use their SHIELD, the faster the results.

As you continue to practice the SHIELD, you will find that your surrounding life changes for the positive as well. All sorts of wonderful things can happen, so watch what you ask for!

The basic premise behind this work is that if you assume you are loved, you will attract love. If you assume you are not loved, you will not attract love, and even if you do attract it, you may not recognize it when it is right in front of you. Now, you might think to yourself that this doesn't make sense because you do believe you are loved, yet you are not in a good relationship or in any at all. Or you think that you are loved, yet you hate your job, have insomnia, or are unhappy with your life or body.

Under all these circumstances, if you dig into the assumptions that lie hidden in your unconscious, you will undoubtedly find that you actually believe you are not enough or do not have enough.

For this reason, to create a sustainable foundation of beliefs and assumptions, to be happier and healthier over the long term, you ultimately need a new structure for your life to hold and reinforce your SHIELD and Active Belief System. I call this new life structure the Love Pyramid. As you continue reading, you will learn how it works.

5

BUILDING YOUR LOVE PYRAMID

Social Love

Imagine that you live in a place built to your specifications of happiness, comfort, and inspiration. Its walls are thick enough to protect you but decorated with photos of those you love and art that delights your eye. The floors are covered with thick carpeting that cushions your step. The rafters contain a large skylight that fills the house with sun during the day and opens to the stars and universe at night.

Welcome to the Love Pyramid, a life structure that helps you deal with life's stresses, sustains your needs, and assists your growth. As briefly mentioned in the last chapter, your Love Pyramid is composed of Social Love, the love received and given between yourself and others; Self-Love, the nurturance, respect, and love you provide to yourself; and Spiritual Love, your connection to all of life, the universe, to all that is, seen and unseen.

Every aspect of your Love Pyramid is important. Each aspect of love feeds into and strengthens the others. The more you develop any aspect of your Love Pyramid, the more your life structure will grow more resilient, solid, and unbreakable.

SOCIAL LOVE: THE BASE OF THE PYRAMID

The base of your Love Pyramid is Social Love. This surprises some people. How can you love anyone else if you do not love yourself first? Social Love serves as the base of your Love Pyramid because your connection with other people defines what it means to be human.

Think about it: How would you like to live in this world all by yourself? No friends. No loving family. Nobody to go out with. Nobody to call when you are frustrated. No one. All alone.

Dismal.

The love between you and others sustains you and gives your life reason and meaning. The love between you and others not only helps you feel alive, it keeps you alive. Of course, without the intimacy between two people, you would not exist.

But Social Love is the base of the Love Pyramid for one major reason: learning to give love to and receive love from others serves as a model for giving and receiving love to and from yourself and Spirit. When you are born, you do not know what the self is. You learn about yourself only from other people, from the way they treat you.

You learn that you are worthy when others treat you with kindness and respect. You learn that you are good at something when you get a pat on the back for a job well done. You learn about self-forgiveness and self-acceptance by forgiving and accepting others. You learn that you are a part of something larger than yourself when you spend time with friends and loved ones who remind you that you are not alone. You become more empowered and connected when you reach out and help others.

Above all, Social Love affords you affection—holding, embracing, physical tenderness, and a gentle, caring touch given and received—which is a huge factor in keeping the Fear Response in check. When your Fear Response is at bay, your Love Response is able to overcome pain and limitations, nurturing and strengthening you at all levels.

GLORIA: *Fear of Affection*

Gloria, an attractive single woman in her mid-thirties, came to see me, complaining of lower back pain, low energy, and feeling overwrought with emotional problems. She was worried that she had no capacity for intimacy, and she blamed this on her weight. She felt insecure about her body and believed no one would want to be with her, let alone touch her. She often felt insecure, uncomfortable in her own body or in her surroundings.

During those times, she felt she was too serious and closed down; she would not reach out or let anyone reach in. She reported that she rarely let anyone touch her, including her family, and she worried that she would never meet a good man, never get married, and never have a family of her own. She was worried that her biological clock would tick away and she would end up lonely and childless.

I inquired about Gloria's childhood and upbringing. She told me that she had grown up in a male-dominated household. Her father, a wonderful and powerful person, had always had the final and only word. He was always "right," and everyone else, including her mother, was invariably "wrong." She admitted to being scared of him, so that she shied away from him when he asked for a hug. In addition, her mother was not very demonstrative, as she rarely hugged Gloria or told her she was loved. Instead, her mother was critical.

On the one hand, Gloria admitted, it was wonderful to know that her father supported her. On the other hand, she always worried that she would do something "wrong." Her pattern was therefore to refer to him for approval and affirmation, rather than believing in herself. In spite of her desire for approval, she never really listened to what her father told her. They argued constantly, like two bulls going head to head, charging at each other, trying to assert who was stronger, who was better, who was right. To Gloria, it appeared that to win, to be right, to be better, she had to forcefully express her opinions, as he did. She had to show more masculine characteristics to succeed, because, as she saw it, her mother never "won."

Gloria developed a distorted view of what it meant to be a strong woman and what it meant to have an equal relationship with a man. As she did not see her mother acting affectionately, she came to believe that hugging or any form of affectionate touch was unnecessary. She also developed a warped view of her own self-worth. She grew to believe that to succeed in a man's world, she had to coat her heart with armor and not let anyone in. As a result, she found herself isolated and lonely. To ease these feelings, she ate—a lot.

After listening to herself tell her story, Gloria understood that her childhood conditioning lacked affection. Though her parents loved and cared for her, they did not demonstrate their love with affection or instill in her the feeling that she was a lovable person, perfect as she was. I explained to Gloria that it would be necessary to reintroduce this experience. I instructed her to begin to receive touch in a safe way, through such modalities as massage, Reiki, or other forms of energy healing. I instructed her to look in the mirror every day and hug herself, acknowledging that she was loved, lovable, and perfect as she was. She was also to do this every time she felt a compulsive urge to eat.

Two weeks later, Gloria returned. She told me about a huge argument she had had with her father, who had been nagging her that it was time for her to marry and have children. Gloria did not appreciate the reminder that she was approaching the tail end of her childbearing years, and an argument ensued. "I felt like a scared little girl who just wanted to be held, but I was still yelling back at my father," she said. She was so upset that she was ready to rush out of the house, just to get away from the emotional pain she was feeling. Just then, her sister returned from an errand and asked what was wrong. Gloria explained what had happened, and her sister embraced her. Gloria responded by letting her, which was a very new experience for her. Then her father came into the room. He was distressed to see Gloria upset. He too came up to her, embraced her, and said, "I had no idea you were so upset. I never meant to hurt you. I love you; you know that, don't you? I am so proud of you. Please never forget that." Gloria let him hold her and let herself be comforted, as if for the first time, trying not to hear the voice inside her that was continuously saying "You are a terrible person." Instead, she listened to the words of her father. She allowed herself to relax into his embrace and feel safe and loved.

Upon discovering how good a real hug felt, Gloria could not get enough. She began hugging her friends and family on a regular basis. It wasn't just the hugs, though, that helped Gloria feel better. It was really the whole process of acknowledging that unconsciously she felt bad about herself, learning how to be vulnerable enough to open up to talk about it, and receiving love and support. Gloria began understanding that she was worthy of receiving love and that when she did allow this love in, she also took better care of herself—eating more healthfully, exercising more, getting adequate sleep, and spending more time with people who cared about her. Over time, she began losing weight and feeling less anxious, and her back pain resolved.

SOCIAL LOVE SUPPORTS SELF-LOVE

You learn you are worthy through the repeated experience of love and affection with others. As you feel validated, your Fear Response stays dormant and self-care substitutes for self-destructive behaviors.

Now, what if you have not experienced an abundance of love, affection, and validation in your life? Or you are currently so emotionally distressed that you have forgotten how it feels? If you are going through a contentious divorce or dealing with emotional loss, being loved and supported may seem like a distant memory.

The beauty of the Love Response is that it reprograms the experience of love and nurturance into your subconscious. Even if you have never received validation for who you are, the Love Response will create it within you. By the time you are done with this program, you will know the experience of loving and being loved.

HAVING SOMEONE TO LEAN ON

The positive rewards of Social Love are stored in your memory and integrated into the brain. After repeated positive experiences of Social Love, you develop the self-assurance that you will have someone to lean on or support you in a time of need. The more this occurs, the more likely that the primitive lizard brain and other brain regions involved in the Fear Response will stay dormant until they are really needed. The less active the Fear Response, the healthier and happier you are and the more likely you are to engage and share love with others. Then you can develop supportive relationships.

Research shows that involvement in healthy and supportive relationships improves an individual's coping skills, psychological and physical health, and chances for prolonged survival.[1] A study of older adults with diabetes found a strong association with social support and mortality, with a 41 percent decreased risk of death in those individuals with medium levels of support and a 55 percent decreased risk in those with high levels of support.[2]

On the other hand, the absence of positive social interaction is associated with physical and mental illness. Studies show that lonely individuals cope with the same type of stress less effectively than social individuals. One study found that socially active individuals were more likely to seek support, view stress as less threatening, and find meaning in what was happening. Furthermore, these individuals tended to be healthier than the lonely individuals.[3] Another study evaluated social isolation in the elderly and the effects of social support intervention on their health. The data showed that social support significantly improved depression and physical health in the elderly.

In addition, researchers found that wounds take longer to heal in patients who have been involved in an argument with a loved one and in married couples who do not get along.[4] It never fails to amaze me that each time my patients improve their social circle, their health improves.

 SARAH: *Finding Friends*

Sarah was thirty-eight years old when she first came to see me. She complained of insomnia, chronic back pain, and anxiety. She often self-medicated with alcohol. Her symptoms had been present for many years but had recently gotten worse when her long-term boyfriend decided to move to another state to pursue his career.

Sarah admitted that she once had a lot of friends, but over the years, she had lost touch with them. She became dependent on her boyfriend, spending little time with other people, even though her boyfriend would often spend time out with his friends or colleagues. She complained that she was scared of being alone and very upset that she had given up everything to be with this man, who was basically abandoning her to build his career.

I encouraged Sarah to reconnect with old friends and to join her local synagogue, which was frequented by younger people. She found that her friends had missed her and that many people in her age group at her synagogue shared her interests. She felt "alive" again and back to her "old self." Sarah soon began developing a stronger social network, so that by the time her boyfriend left for a different state, she was less upset than she expected. She understood that she had based her expectations of being happy on the actions or presence of her boyfriend, not understanding that being happy came from feeling good about herself and from being around people (not just one person) who love and care for you. As she grew to feel better about herself and her life, Sarah found she slept better, her back pain went away, and she was rarely anxious. No alcohol required.

FRIENDS FOR HEALTH

Why does having friends improve your health? Developing social contacts provides you with the sense of feeling safe and secure, lessening your Fear Response and its symptoms.

Imagine this:

You have just started a job and you are going to your first work-related social function. You are so new that you are still in the process of learning your coworkers' names. You are going to the party alone, and the one person whom you do know from work can't make the event.

What kinds of sensations do you notice in your body?

What kinds of thoughts race through your mind?

Now imagine that your friend from work decides not only to go to this function but to accompany you. In fact, she offers to personally take you around and introduce you to everyone at the party.

Now what kind of sensations or thoughts do you notice?

Improved social support provides reward and comfort, pleasurable experiences, and a basis for feeling secure to face your challenges. If you think about it, you are more likely to relax and let down your guard, if you know someone else is around keeping an eye out for possible danger. Social support and interactions also serve as stimulants for your personal growth, self-concept and identity, and ability to make meaning of the hardships in your life. Within the brain, this translates into new nerve growth, more memories of positive outcomes and pleasant experiences, less Fear Response activation, and healthier emotions, thoughts, beliefs, and attitudes that promote better health and well-being, the direct results of positive physiology.

A simple exercise to do when you are feeling alone or nervous is the "Feel the Love Response" exercise you learned at the end of Chapter 2, when you imagined the face of someone you love.

EXERCISE

Feel the Love Response

Get yourself comfortable.

Close your eyes.

Imagine the face of someone you love.

See their face smiling at you.

Notice everything about them.

Notice how this makes you feel.

As you breathe in deeply and exhale completely, notice how you feel.

The more you practice this visualization, the more you will assimilate the feeling of love that this person affords you, and the less alone you will feel.

PETS AND HEALTH

Your emotional support comes largely from people, but the support people receive from pets has proven surprisingly profound and mirrors some of the elements of human relationships that contribute to health and well-being.

Studies show that pets reduce the Fear Response. Dr. Johannes Odendaal, for instance, found that positive human-pet contact led to a release of neurochemicals in both humans and pets. In addition, cortisol levels dropped in humans who spent time with pets, indicating that pets help reduce stress.[5] Dr. Karen Allen looked at cardiovascular reactivity (blood pressure and heart rate) of 240 married couples, half of whom owned a pet. The results showed that people with pets had lower cardiovascular reactivity than those without pets at baseline, smaller increases during stress, and faster recovery after the stress.[6]

Since pets offer what many humans cannot—unconditional love and companionship—it is not surprising that they can help regulate the Fear Response in humans and also help enhance mood. Do you own a pet? In my experiences, somehow, both my cat and my dog know exactly when I am in need of more affection. Before anyone can even register that I am upset, there is my cat or dog, putting its head on my lap, reminding me that I am loved and cherished.

Individuals who own pets are not only less lonely and depressed, they also live longer. This is especially true of the elderly. Studies show that pets lower blood pressure, raise endorphins, and reduce the need for pain medications.[7] Introducing pet visits into nursing homes improves the mood, spirit, and energy of the residents.[8] Seniors who have pets see the doctor far less often than those who don't, according to a study of nearly one thousand Medicare patients by University of California at Los Angeles.[9]

Pets not only offer unconditional love, they remind you of hope and prompt you to anticipate the future. They help you feel alive and look forward to what might come next.

Lucy and Caroline: *Something to Live For*

Lucy was seventy-eight when she and her daughter, Caroline, came to see me. Caroline was worried that Lucy was dying from some devastating medical condition such as cancer. She felt that Lucy's doctors were not trying hard enough to find the cause of her illness. Lucy had lost an extreme amount of weight, had no appetite, was perpetually short of breath, and spoke little. Her daughter wanted her mom back.

Lucy did indeed appear frail and weak. She needed assistance walking to my office and was easily winded from the short walk.

I went through Lucy's medical record, and contrary to her daughter's claim, it was clear to me that Lucy's doctors had indeed done a thorough medical workup. According to the records, there was no medical explanation for her condition aside from possible depression, for which they had started Lucy on Prozac.

I asked if Lucy had experienced any loss in the past year. Caroline told me her father had died several years ago. Lucy had lived alone for many years and had been doing just fine. She could think of no one else whom her mom might have been close to who had died or taken ill in the past year.

I rephrased my question and asked if Lucy had experienced loss of any kind—such as a friend who had moved away, or perhaps Lucy had made some sort of move. Or perhaps there had been an anniversary of a wedding or even a death at the time Lucy's symptoms had started.

This time Lucy answered, telling me that she had moved to an assisted living home a year before I met her. She had made the move when taking care of her house became difficult but she still wanted to be independent. Caroline then chimed in that Lucy's symptoms had started right around the time of her wedding anniversary. In fact, they had begun the first time that Lucy was not living in the marital home.

Hearing her daughter's words, Lucy started crying.

After comforting Lucy, I spoke with Caroline separately and asked if Lucy had ever had a dog or a cat for a pet. She had, when her kids were young. I encouraged Caroline to get her mother a dog. I advised her to start slowly, by bringing the dog to her mother for visits to see how Lucy reacted. If all went well and the assisted living home allowed it, Lucy could then keep the dog as her pet.

Lucy instantly fell in love with Liza, a mutt of some sort, and looked forward to her visits. Lucy began to eat more, gained back the weight she had lost, and, most important, rediscovered her smile and zest for life.

One of the reasons, I believe, that Lucy got better was that a pet gave her life meaning again. She could now receive and give unconditional love.

You might ask the question, then, why Lucy didn't simply volunteer and help others? As you will learn later in the chapter on Spiritual Love, this likely would have helped her. However, when you are running on empty, you often have little to share. You don't quickly make the intellectual leap that giving to others might be just what you need. Even if you can make this connection intellectually, when you're running on empty it can be difficult to motivate yourself to volunteer. Pets provide an easy and immediate opportunity for receiving and giving love.

RECEIVING AS WELL AS GIVING

Social Love requires asking for help and giving help, building community and relying on community, supporting and being supported, giving and receiving love. For many, supporting others is easy. The problem comes in accepting support from others. In some way, they have come to view asking for help as "bad," as a show of failure and vulnerability. Truth is, you need to receive. Otherwise, it is like giving the entire community water from your well without ever taking a drink yourself.

THINK ABOUT IT

- How many times do I actually ask for help?
- Would I even know how to accept help if it came knocking at my door?
- Am I so busy being fearful, angry, or alone that I cannot relax long enough to be aware of what my needs are or to realize that support is available for me?
- On the other hand, am I so wrapped up in myself and my own problems that I cannot see through to the needs of others?
- How many times do I find myself in one too many imbalanced relationships and situations?

You want your well of love to overflow so that there is plenty to go around for you and everyone else. Remember the dynamics of life—that for every up there is a down; for every day, there is a night; for everything you give, you have the need to receive and vice versa. In this way, you create a cycle that is in balance and flow.

You create what I call a circle of love.

The Circle of Love

Just as your breath involves inhaling and exhaling, Social Love involves both receiving and giving love. In and out, the circle of love, like the circle of your breath, is never-ending.

No matter how much you exhale, your body knows you will always get more oxygen when you inhale. The circle of love is similar—more love is always on its way. If for any reason the flow of love in your life is disrupted or out of balance, panic and fear can take over, just as though someone were cutting off your air supply. A life devoid of love—whether given or received—is a terrifying proposition, but this much I know: as long as there is breath in your body, you can strengthen and balance your circle of love and defuse the fear that you will not have enough.

Try It

Breathe in and try holding your breath.
How long can you do it? Forty-five seconds? Ninety? Not
    forever, that's for sure.

As soon as you let go of your breath, a new one comes in. Just like that. You have no fear of letting go of your breath because you know another one will replace it at the right time.

What if you had the same attitude toward everything in your life? You know you can spend $100 because another $100 will soon replenish it. Or you know you can let go of one job because another job would start. Being whole is not a fixed state but one that is constantly changing, giving, and receiving, always in flux yet always complete.

Just like your breath.

THE LOVE CIRCLE BREATH EXERCISE

Sit in a comfortable position.
Pay attention to your breath.
Focus on the inhalation.
Inhale deeply.
Focus on the exhalation.
Exhale completely.
Notice how much air you can take in before you feel as
    though your chest is about to explode.
Notice how easily you can let it go.
Notice how you cannot hold on to your breath even if
    you try.
You have no choice but to let it go.
Notice how when you exhale completely, your inhalation
    begins immediately.
Notice that there is no way to stop the cycle.
Notice how every time you let go of your breath, a new
    breath comes in.
Focus on your chest as the breath moves in and out.
Imagine that you are breathing in love.
Let go. Imagine that as you exhale you are sharing this love
    with someone you care about. As you exhale, they inhale
    your love.
As they exhale, you inhale their love.
Do this for at least ten breaths.

The flow of the circle of breath mirrors the flow of the circle of love. Every ancient wisdom tradition tells us that love is always around us. It is the energy of the universe, the life force within all creatures, the constant in our lives. Through building your Love Pyramid, you will come to understand and trust this universal truth.

LOVE CIRCLES

Like the air you breathe, love is available to you at all times. It circulates in and out, within you and around you, between you and another person, among many people, throughout the earth and ultimately the entire cosmos. This love circle is constant, ever-flowing, everlasting, and always complete when it is in balance.

The love circle, like your breath, is in balance when love flows evenly, when receiving and giving are equal. Just as you inhale and exhale, you receive and disperse love. You cannot hold on to it even if you try.

As love flows from you, it can go anywhere—to another person, a community, nature, or a divine spirit. The love then returns to you from those same sources, completing the circle. The constant and simultaneous circle of giving and receiving takes many forms, the most obvious, tangible, fulfilling, and challenging of which are our interpersonal relationships.

Building strong relationships creates a solid foundation for your Love Pyramid and keeps the circle of love in balance. In the next two chapters, you will learn what can inhibit you from good relationships, how to overcome these obstacles, and how to create the relationships you want.

6

Social Love

Creating the Base of Your Love Pyramid

Social Love—the love and affection that you give and receive throughout your life—supports your everyday existence. It is your foundation, your cushion that props you up in the knowledge that you have enough and will have enough love and support when you need it. It helps you escape the frame of mind that love is scarce in your life and assures you that love is abundant and available to you always.

Just as you need to breathe in and breathe out, you also need to give and receive love to and from others. When you don't, for whatever reason, your life tips out of balance and the Fear Response takes over. To build a solid base for your Love Pyramid, I will help you tune in to what's working and what's not in the Social Love areas of your life. Your mission is to meet these goals:

1. Develop awareness of when you are giving too much or taking too much in a relationship.
2. Learn to trust that love is available to you.
3. Transform your anger by having compassion for yourself.
4. Allow yourself to receive love and heal your heart.

Once you meet these goals, you will feel the flow of love in your life as a cushion against fear and stress. Being in the flow of love means not being in resistance, which means not being in stress, which means not being in fear. Fear can make you hold your breath or not breathe at all. The same thing can occur with love. You can either give too much or not let enough in. The consequence is an emotional depletion that leads to physical discomfort and disease.

Goal 1: Develop awareness of when you are giving too much or taking too much in a relationship.

Let's start with a familiar scenario.

It's been a hard day at work. You are exhausted. You arrive home and just want to chill for a while. Instead, one minute after you walk in the door, your spouse asks, "What's for dinner?"

You lose it. "Why am I the one who always has to make dinner? Why do I have to do everything around here? Why can't you make dinner for a change? Why can't I be taken care of once in a while?"

Your spouse, fending off the attack, yells back that he or she had a hard day and can't deal with your mood. You both storm off to separate parts of the house, angry, feeling misunderstood, unsupported, and hungry.

What can you learn from this example?

ARE YOU A GIVER OR A TAKER?

Neither of you could see beyond your own fears and anger so you could communicate in a way that would support the other and perhaps solve the problem. Both of you wanted to receive, and neither wanted to give. The more each of you did not receive, the more you lost trust that love was available for you, heightening your anger or fear. In your mind, you are the one who always gives and does not receive. But is this really true?

Let's find out.

QUESTIONS FOR YOU: AM I A GIVER OR A TAKER?

- How often are you able to say "no" to people?
- Is it your responsibility to make sure everyone is happy or act as peacekeeper?
- Do you feel it reflects badly on you if you don't make others happy?

- Does it seem as though you are always the one who is in need and asking for help?
- Are you the one always listening to your friends' problems but rarely telling them about yours?
- Do you need to be the center of attention the majority of the time, or can you share the stage?

The truth is, in different relationships you may adopt different roles. Often you can be a giver or a taker in the same relationship, depending on the situation.

Usually, the issue of whether you are a giver or a taker arises during a disagreement or time of tension, as in the example above. Think back to a time when you were upset or in conflict with a partner or an individual.

Ask yourself the following questions:

- What thoughts of fear, resentment, or anger raced through my mind?
- In what ways did this situation prompt me to feel that I do not have enough or will not have enough? How did this situation cause me to feel insecure?
- What did I want from this person?
- What caused me to believe that my wants or needs would not be met in this situation?
- What can I do about it? What scares me from doing something about it?
- Am I looking at this situation or this relationship clearly?

Being aware of whether you are a giver or a taker is not a judgment or indictment of yourself. It is simply a reflection of how you perceive yourself in your world. It is a product of your unconscious mind assuming that your foundation of love is too weak to support you. As a giver, you perceive that you will not be loved unless you give. You often find yourself upset that you are not being appreciated, supported, or loved enough in return. As a taker, you are never convinced that you are loved and supported. With either negative belief, you cannot deeply trust that you will be okay now or in the future. So you find yourself in imbalanced relationships where you feel like you are not enough or where the other person is not enough for you.

What do you do to correct the imbalance in your relationships? You learn to trust.

Goal 2: *Learn to trust that love is available to you.*

FEAR VERSUS TRUST

Imagine: You are a child, seeing everything for the first time, curious, excited, and fully engaged in playing, listening, feeling, tasting, and smelling. You pay attention to everything around you and within you. You live in the space not yet touched by human experience.

How do we get from there to here, from the open air and sunshine of childhood to the stuffy rooms and closed doors of adult life?

As you grew up, like most people, you experienced hurt and disappointment. Over time, you created boundaries and barriers to protect yourself from further injury. You developed conscious and unconscious fear of what you could not understand or control. You lost trust that you would always have enough or be enough. Distrust became part of your internal programming.

LEARNING TO TRUST

The first step in trusting is to notice that you distrust; to identify that you feel fear and the circumstances that trigger it. For instance, you may not trust that anyone really listens to you. Or you do not trust that you will ever have enough money or that you will find true love.

Here is how my patient David learned.

 DAVID: *Developing Trust*

When I first met him, David was thirty-eight and complained of chronic back pain and anxiety. He had difficulty holding on to a job. Either he was fired or he quit each job, saying that he didn't get along with management. He had even more difficulty staying in a committed relationship. Each relationship ended because he was "rejected." He later admitted that he was usually rejected because he had affairs with other women. In each of his relationships, he admitted, the women were really good people who did nothing but give to him. When I asked him why he acted as he did, he replied, "I would have been rejected sooner or later anyway. I am not good enough for any of them, really. I figure I might as well have a good time now and cut my losses, beat them to the punch."

At this point, it seemed to me that probably since his early childhood, David had developed the belief that he was unlovable and that he was always going to be rejected. From my experience, fear related to survival often manifests with lower back pain. I suspected that David's childhood history had taught him he could not trust that he would always be taken care of and safe.

David's early years were indeed very traumatic. His father abandoned the family when David was an infant. His family then lived in poverty, and his mother, to overcome her grief, turned to alcohol. Many days she did not come home, and David remembered hiding under his bed when he was five years old, waiting for his mother to arrive. When she did not, David and his siblings would often roam around the neighborhood, looking for food. He and his siblings eventually spent much of their childhood moving from one foster home to another. Every time David was relocated, he would reinvent himself, pretending he was someone different, so that he would be liked. He was sure that in reality he was no good and therefore it was better to hide his true identity.

David did not trust that he would ever have or be enough. He became a "taker." In order to heal, he had to learn to build a foundation of love that helped him trust and believe that love would stick around, that he was worthy of being loved.

I asked David to practice the SHIELD anytime he felt bad—physically or emotionally. I gave him visualizations that involved imagining that he was connected to the love of the earth and that he was receiving unconditional love from the people he cared about, especially from his grandmother, with whom he was very close. We used positive verbal commands that he could say to himself to help him feel more supported, such as "I trust that I am loved and supported." I instructed David to practice listening to people without jumping to conclusions and, when talking to his friends, letting them know when he was feeling down. These were his first steps toward building trust and creating his foundation of love. Eventually, he found a job that he loved and developed a group of friends who support his business and his life.

Your Love Rx for Appreciating Yourself

AWARENESS EXERCISE

The goal of the following exercise is to guide you to an awareness of your level of trust or distrust of others.

Part 1: Awareness of Trust and Distrust

Read through the following trust questions and ask yourself, Do I trust that:

- I will always have enough money?
- I will always have enough food?
- I will always have my health?
- I will always have my friends?
- I will never be alone?
- I will always succeed?
- I will always have what I need?
- I will be loved even if I do not do what is expected or wanted of me?

Pick one or two of the questions, then follow the instructions below.

- After choosing a question, close your eyes, repeat the question, and contemplate your answer. Notice how you feel.
- How does your chest feel?
- What are you doing with your breath?
- Pay attention to the rest of your body, especially your spine, noticing any twinges of discomfort.
- Notice emotions that might come up for you—agitation, sense of calm, sadness, fear, and so on.
- Jot down your answers.

Part 2: The Release

The following steps will help you work through your reactions to these questions.

1. Choose one or more of the questions for which your answer was "no."
2. Without putting any pressure on yourself (no one is judging what you write, and no one will read this but you), begin to write freely about your answer. Set a timer for five minutes. If you find yourself on a roll, reset the timer and keep going.
3. You may find that the word you keep writing over and over again is "because." Try digging deeper after each "because" to find all the "becauses" that may precede it. (Example: Because that makes me sad; because I don't like to be sad.)
4. Some of your answers may sound excruciatingly juvenile, simple-minded, or whiney. That's okay. Whatever you are writing is valid. Just keep going. Take this opportunity to complain and whine! This is just your child-self expressing its needs. Perhaps you will find yourself going back in time, to an experience in your early life. When the timer goes off, stop.
5. Once you have finished, place your hands on the words and repeat, "I now release you from my body." You may wish to destroy the paper—shred or burn it—as a ritual for releasing your past. The point is to remove your attachment to your fears and to the memories that no longer serve you.

Now do the following exercise.

Part 3: Healing Distrust

Hopefully you are discovering that there exists a source to your fears or lack of trust. Your job now is to reprogram that distrust into trust.

Daily Reprogramming Tool to Build Trust
1. Sit or lie down in a comfortable position.
   Close your eyes.
   Inhale deeply.
   Exhale completely.

Continue inhaling deeply and exhaling completely throughout the exercise.

After at least five complete breaths, create your SHIELD.

A divine light now surrounds you and holds you. By "divine light" I am referring to a light that holds everything that is pure, loving, and kind. It can be light that comes from the golden rays of the sun or from the white glow of a star.

Imagine that inside the SHIELD of divine light, the images of a divine mother and a divine father stand right there beside you. Again, "divine" refers to all that is pure, loving, warm, and compassionate. These divine beings embody these virtues. You can imagine them simply as images composed of light who are full of unconditional love just for you.

As your divine parents hold you, cradle you, and rock you, they repeat the following Trust Prayer:

THE TRUST PRAYER
> Trust.
> Trust that you are not alone.
> Trust that you did nothing wrong.
> Trust that you are loved and lovable.
> That you are the expression of a divine energy.
> And perfect just as you are.

2. Now say the Trust Prayer to yourself.
   Repeat the prayer over and over again, replacing "you" with "I."
   Allow yourself to receive your divine mother and father's love.
   Surrender into their arms and let yourself be held, nurtured, and rocked.
   You feel safe. You feel loved.
   You know you are not alone.

3. Now repeat the following positive verbal command silently to yourself:
   "I trust that I am loved and supported."
   Hold this image and repeat these words as long as you wish.

This healing has various components: the visualization of your divine mother and father, the Trust Prayer, and the positive verbal command. Using all or any of these components will benefit you.

You can practice these exercises throughout your day to help build your foundation of trust. The key to success here is repetition. The more you practice all or any of the components of the Trust Healing, the more you activate your Love Response.

- When a friend asks you to do her a favor for which you know you have no time. You feel you cannot say "no" because she is in such a bad state herself. The situation is causing you anxiety and feelings of guilt.
- When you feel that someone is taking you for granted. You are afraid to say anything for fear others may get mad or possibly leave you.
- When you are overwhelmed by responsibility but feel you cannot show you are needy. You think people see you as the "strong one," the one whom others rely on. You fear others might "fall apart" or may not want to be friends with you anymore if they cannot rely on you.
- When you are afraid to tell someone how you feel because you think he or she may get angry.
- When you are afraid you are going to fail or are not good enough.
- When you are worried that you do not have enough of something, such as you do not have enough money, support, or time.

Goal 3: Transform your anger by having compassion for yourself.

DISTRUST AND ANGER

When you feel loved, other people's actions and behaviors bother you less, and you are more likely to feel compassion and forgiveness toward their actions than anger and resentment. Everyone possesses the capacity to understand, forgive, and love unconditionally—it's just a matter of clearing the anger and negativity from your system.

Think about a time when you felt wonderful, perhaps a time when you fell in love or had great success at work or play. Your heart felt open and full, and you seemed to have a permanent smile on your face. Almost nothing bothered you.

Now recall the opposite scenario—a time when you felt tired, overwhelmed, or unhappy about the way you looked or felt. Did you have the same capacity for understanding, forgiveness, or compassion? Did more things and most people annoy you or irritate you?

Anger is natural and normal. The problem arises when anger controls you and your actions, when your Fear Response takes over and either harms you or triggers you to hurt others.

How can you rise above anger and extinguish the Fear Response? How can you use anger to motivate you into positive action and not lose your balance? You can do this by searching for the underlying cause of your anger.

Often, the root of your anger is the notion that you have not received enough compassion or forgiveness yourself and therefore lack a model for how to give those qualities to others.

If you can give yourself what you lack, you can move through your anger. You can allow yourself to receive love and compassion.

 EMMA: *Finding Compassion*

When I met Emma, she was thirty-seven and had been preparing to move into a new home for the past month, while working two jobs. She did not ask for help. She believed no one could really help her but found herself feeling bitter and overwhelmed nonetheless. To top it off, her back was in spasm.

Emma recalled that her back had gone into spasm while packing. She had dropped to her knees in pain, not believing what was happening. It could not have happened at a worse time. She had so much to do. The move was scheduled for the following day! That was when she decided to come see me.

I commented that perhaps her back was trying to tell her something. I asked Emma to tune in to the base of her spine and then ask her back why it was causing her so much pain.

Emma closed her eyes and began first noting how the lower spine felt and the emotions she was experiencing. She noted that her spine felt weak and that she had the sensation of being overwhelmed. I instructed her to ask her back if it felt loved and supported, and Emma answered that it had replied, "No, I feel alone. There is no one to help me. It isn't fair."

I instructed Emma to bring her awareness to the muscles in her back and notice how they protected the spine; to notice that since the spine was weak, the muscles were tightening in the attempt to support her. Perplexed, Emma asked, "But why if they act to protect me, do they end up hurting me? Why go into spasm now?"

"Why do you think? You did not feel loved and supported. How did that make you feel?" I asked Emma. "Angry," she answered. I then asked her, "What do muscles do when people are angry?" "Tighten," she replied.

Her eyes lit up in understanding. Instantly she recalled how frustrated she had been all week, that she had faced one complication after another and had no one to help her. She even recalled yelling at her family for not helping her.

I explained to Emma that first she would want to address her anger and accept it as a normal reaction to a stressful and frustrating situation. She also needed to acknowledge that her anger stemmed from a distorted belief that she was not loved or supported. She needed to give herself love and compassion, and then, perhaps, she might feel better.

I instructed Emma to imagine that the divine light from her SHIELD was filling her heart with compassion for herself and her imperfections. I had her repeat the positive verbal command "I trust that I am loved and supported" and imagine the divine parents holding her and comforting her. I repeated the Trust Prayer with her.

At her next visit, Emma told me that as she practiced the SHIELD, her Cushion of Love healing exercise, the Trust Prayer, and positive verbal commands, her spasms began to subside. She recalled that the first time she had done this process at home, her spasms had lessened in intensity within about ten minutes. Then, as if by some plan, the phone started ringing with calls from Emma's family and friends, concerned and wanting to help. As she continued to use her reprogramming tools, more of her friends and family offered to help and she became aware of how much people actually did love and support her.

At her next visit, Emma said she had no pain at all. She understood that feeling compassion for herself and the circumstances and allowing love into her life strengthened her foundation of love. She was then able to let go of her anger and feel better.

Your Love Rx for Transforming Anger

AWARENESS EXERCISE

Part 1: Awareness of Anger

> Set a timer for ten to fifteen minutes.
> Close your eyes.
> Inhale deeply.
> Exhale completely.
> Create your SHIELD of loving divine light all around you.
> Re-create the image in your mind of someone who made you
>   angry—who wronged you in some way, betrayed you,
>   took you for granted, or hurt you.
> Try to get a clear image of this person or situation in your
>   mind.
> Let negative emotions rise up through your body. They will
>   not destroy you.
> Let yourself be angry, scared, upset, grief-stricken.
> If you need to cry, cry.
> If you need to scream, scream.
> Do not hold back. You are safe.
> Observe as the feelings rise.
> What do you want to do or see yourself doing to this person
>   in this situation? Do you want to inflict harm?
> Do not feel bad if you do; just observe what you are feeling,
>   as if you are watching a movie of your life.
> Ask yourself questions and listen for answers.
> Why are you angry or upset?
> Why haven't you been able to forgive this person?
> Why did they do what they did to you?
> Ask and listen.
> When the timer goes off open your eyes.

Part 2: The Release

Reset the timer for fifteen minutes.

1. Write why you were or are angry. Write what you saw and felt. Write why you cannot forgive. Write without thinking too much, judging, or holding back.
2. You may draw a picture of yourself and the person or thing that is making you feel angry and add adjectives to describe how they have made you feel. Use expletives if you need to! Do not hold back.
3. When the timer goes off, place your hands on the words and say, "I now release you from my body." Then destroy the paper.

Doing this exercise one time may not sufficiently release all of your anger. If this is the case, you can continue with your anger release, journaling for the next three to seven days, always making sure that you set the timer. In this way, you learn how not to ruminate, how to allow yourself to have anger, work through it, release it, and then pick up where you left off another day. Always finish up this exercise with Part 3: Filling Yourself with Compassion. At some point when you sit down to do this exercise, you will find that the anger is no longer there.

Part 3: The Healing: Filling Yourself with Compassion

Close your eyes.

Inhale deeply.

Exhale completely.

Set the intention to let go of thoughts, worries, stress, and fears as you exhale.

Exhale, let go. You do not need to know specifically what is blocking you; just set the intention to let it go as you exhale.

Create your SHIELD of divine light.

Imagine the divine parents in the SHIELD holding and comforting you.

Imagine that as you inhale, the light from your SHIELD melts into your chest, so that your chest fills with light and compassion.

Exhale. Feel the light and compassion spread throughout your chest.

Inhale. Feel your chest fill with light and compassion.

Exhale. Feel the light and compassion spread throughout your chest.

Repeat these words silently to yourself over and over again: "I trust that I am loved and supported and I am worthy of receiving love."

Inhale. Feel your chest fill with light and compassion.

Exhale. Feel light and compassion spread throughout your chest.

Inhale as the divine light fills your heart with compassion and love.

Exhale as the light and compassion spread out of your chest and extend out to anyone or anywhere that you wish.

Do this for at least twenty cycles.

Daily Reprogramming Tools for Anger

WHAT TO DO
- Create the SHIELD.
- Imagine your divine parents standing in your SHIELD, holding you and comforting you.
- Repeat the Trust Prayer.
- Imagine the divine light filling your heart with compassion.
- Repeat the positive verbal command "I trust that I am loved and supported and I am worthy of receiving love."

If you practice these reprogramming tools repeatedly, you will find, over time, that you feel calmer, more patient, and more loving.

WHEN TO USE THE REPROGRAMMING TOOLS
- When you feel angry, resentful, or frustrated.
- When you are in the heat of an argument.
- When someone is rude to you, even someone you do not know (like someone cutting you off in traffic).
- When you feel impatient or annoyed.
- When you feel you have been taken for granted.
- When you are upset that you are not being heard.
- When someone hurts you or offends you.
- When you feel that no one cares about you.

Goal 4: Allow yourself to receive love and heal your heart.

THE HEART IS AT THE HEART OF IT ALL

For centuries, wisdom and spiritual traditions have instructed us to "look into our hearts" or "open our hearts," in order to find peace and balance. These phrases are now so common and lacking in real meaning that they have become clichés, the stuff of holiday greeting cards and sappy songs.

Ironically, recent science confirms that the heart indeed does more than just beat and circulate blood to the body. Not only does the heart regulate the fluid and oxygen balance of every organ in the body, but it is closely connected to the emotional response center of the brain called the limbic system. The heart also uses the same neurotransmitters as the brain to function since the majority of heart cells are actually nerve cells. When it feels something, the heart signals the brain to put the feelings into context. The brain then mobilizes other bodily systems to guide your thoughts, behaviors, and actions in response to the given situation.

The heart contains the information from the memories of your lifetime. Joyful experiences, such as the experience of love, elicit pleasant sensations in the heart, positive emotions, stimulating the Love Response. Negative or hurtful experiences feel like wounds in the heart and generate negative emotions, fueling the Fear Response. When you "open your heart" to love using the exercises in this book, you heal your wounds, evoke the Love Response, and find balance and peace.

 NANCY: *Her Heart Problems*

Nancy complained to me of constant chest pain. All her tests, including an EKG, stress test, and sonogram, were normal. The pain felt like a pressure in the middle of her chest, which came on unpredictably.

Having ruled out a medical cause, I delved deeper into her history. I discovered that the chest pain had begun two years earlier, during the time of Nancy's divorce. Recently, the chest pain had gotten worse. When I asked her what had changed or what was different since her chest pain had worsened, Nancy reported that she had been under a lot of stress at work. She did not like her new boss, who was disrespectful and cared only about "numbers." He did not value her or her capabilities and acted as if he did not trust her work. Invariably, she left work feeling angry.

I asked Nancy if there were any similarities between her boss and her ex-husband. She said, "My husband did not value or respect me either."

I then asked Nancy to close her eyes and examine her heart while thinking about her husband, to notice what feelings arose for her. She told me she felt feelings of anger and betrayal. She also started to experience chest pain. I asked her to look at the pain and tell me what she saw. "I see a concrete wall, cold and unmoving, like a wall of armor that will not let anything out or in."

I guided Nancy through creating the SHIELD with the divine parents holding her and comforting her, allowing the light to fill her heart with compassion, and having her repeat the positive verbal command "I trust that I am loved and supported and I am worthy of receiving love." I then taught her the Heart Prayer. As she did this exercise, she told me the concrete wall began to soften. Her pain began to lessen.

Nancy practiced her reprogramming tools for the next three weeks and began to recognize her value on a deeper level. She discovered that she was less bothered by her boss's attitude and behavior. She realized that as long as she sought approval and recognition from others who would or could not give it to her, she would end up feeling angry.

Nancy needed to know, deep in her heart, that she was loved and valued. By seeing the connection between her broken heart and her pain, Nancy was able to see the connection between feeling disrespected, losing trust, and being angry.

Your Love Rx

AWARENESS EXERCISE

Part 1: Awareness of How the Heart Feels

Set a timer for ten to fifteen minutes.
Close your eyes.
Inhale deeply.
Exhale completely.

Create your SHIELD.

Bring your awareness to your chest.

Notice what your chest feels like.

Notice your breath moving in and out.

Notice any sensation in your chest, especially the center of
   your chest. The center of your chest is the heart center.

Notice what the heart center feels like as you breathe in
   and out.

Acknowledge your heart.

Honor your heart.

Introduce yourself.

See if your heart answers back.

Notice any tightness in your heart.

Notice any pain in your heart.

Notice if you do not feel anything at all.

Recall a time when you felt disappointed, betrayed, or hurt.

Ask the heart to show you the wound where your heart shut
   down or closed off in an effort to protect you.

Ask your heart to show you the imagery, the words, or the
   experience.

Perhaps your heart will show you a movie reel of yourself in
   your childhood.

Notice what you see, hear, sense, or feel.

What happened in your past to make you feel this way?

When the timer goes off, stop and open your eyes.

Part 2: The Release

Reset the timer for fifteen minutes.

1. Write down your experience and what you feel. You may find
   that when you initially do this exercise, you do not feel or see
   much. That is okay. You also will find that as you become
   more aware of your heart, this exercise becomes easier. When
   you sit down to write, just see what happens. See what you
   choose to write about. Your instinctive writing will lead you to
   what your heart was trying to show you. Write without judging or stopping. Do not hold back.

2. When the timer goes off, stop. Place your hands on the words

and repeat, "I now release you from my body" and destroy the paper. Follow this exercise with Part 3: The Heart Prayer. As with the anger release, it may take you several times before the heart wound is fully released, so you may want to write in the release journal for three to seven days, always followed by the Heart Prayer below.

Part 3: Healing: The Heart Prayer

Close your eyes.
Inhale deeply.
Exhale completely.
Create your SHIELD with the divine parents holding you
 and comforting you.
Imagine the divine light filling your heart with compassion
 and love.
Inhale as the divine light fills your heart with compassion
 and love.
Exhale as the light and compassion spread throughout your
 chest.
Say the Heart Prayer:

THE HEART PRAYER
 May my heart receive the light today.
 May my heart be open to love.
 May the light touch my heart today
 And open my heart to love.

Inhale as the divine light fills your heart with compassion
 and love.
Exhale as the light and compassion spread throughout your
 chest.
Repeat the Heart Prayer for at least twenty cycles.

Daily Reprogramming Tools for Healing the Heart

WHAT TO DO
 • Create your SHIELD with the divine parents holding you and
  comforting you.

- Imagine divine light filling your heart with compassion and love.
- Say the Heart Prayer.
- Say the positive verbal command "I trust that I am loved and supported and that I am worthy of receiving love."

WHEN TO USE THE REPROGRAMMING TOOLS
- All the time!
- When you feel sad, mad, angry, disappointed, anxious, worried, unsure, ashamed, guilty, etc.
- When you are in an argument.
- When you are about to go on a blind date.
- When you are going on a job interview.
- When you have been pulled into your boss's office.
- When you do not feel listened to or heard.
- When you feel misunderstood.
- When you feel bad, physically, psychologically, or emotionally.

As you use these reprogramming tools, pay attention to what happens in your life. You can say the Trust Prayer or the Heart Prayer or both as you visualize a divine light, compassion, and love filling your heart. You can repeat your positive verbal command continuously throughout the day. You may find not only that you start to feel physically and emotionally better, but that your relationships change. You may notice that there are people you really do not want in your life and others you suddenly do.

In the next chapter, you will learn to use the Social Love basics—developing trust, transforming anger, and opening your heart—to improve your relationships and create a Soul Family.

7

Social Love in Action

Creating Your Soul Family

Imagine you are arguing with your partner after coming home from a hard day of work. You are feeling unsupported, angry, and frustrated.

What if on your way home from work you had created your SHIELD, filled yourself with love and compassion before setting foot in the house. Would you have reacted with such anger toward your partner? Would you have held the same expectations of him or her? Perhaps you might have remained calm. You might have shifted your energy and had a discussion with your partner rather than an argument. You might have ordered Chinese takeout by now or even stopped at the corner deli and picked up dinner for both of you.

Think about it this way: If you walk up to someone with the intention of punching him or her, what do you think the reaction will be? Conversely, if you approach someone with the open arms of love and acceptance, how will that person respond?

Of course, how can you extend loving, open arms to someone when you are feeling angry and hurt?

You could feed yourself some love first, which you have just learned how to do in the previous chapter.

Here is a major characteristic of love: it does not matter where love comes from, where it starts, what its source is—whether it's another person, the self, or Spirit. When you are in need of love, you can reach for the closest building block of your Love Pyramid, get the love that is most accessible to you, and lift yourself up.

If you are in conflict with a partner, you can find love by engaging in the self-nurturing behaviors of self-love. If you are running on empty and cannot muster self-love, you can look to Spirit or nature. If you are feeling bad about yourself, you can turn to your significant other, family, and friends.

Whatever form of love you experience gives you better access to the other forms and strengthens your Love Pyramid overall.

Love builds upon itself, all around you, and as far as you can imagine.

As you receive love—whatever the source—you develop clarity about what you want and don't want in life. With this clarity, you discover whom you can count on in times of need. You create strong and nurturing relationships, in which giving and receiving are equal. As you receive love, you share it with others, creating stronger and greater love circles, which eventually form what I call your Soul Family.

WHAT IS A SOUL FAMILY?

The people in your Soul Family bring out the best in you and support you when your worst appears, as opposed to bringing out the worst in you so that your best part is ignored. Members of your Soul Family support you as you support them. Each person in your Soul Family works on his or her own fears and does not trigger fear in you. For instance, let's say you were telling your friend about a new boyfriend or girlfriend. You have some concerns already, and you want to hash them out with someone.

Two scenarios could take place. If your friend has his or her own problems in relationships, he or she may impose his or her insecurities on the conversations and point out all the things that you are doing wrong, thus increasing your anxiety. A person with a more balanced approach to relationships and less personal issues about them would talk you through your fears and help you feel more supported. He or she would be aware that some of the issues you are experiencing are the same ones he or she has experienced, and the two of you could find solutions together.

Your Soul Family may or may not include your actual family members. It depends on whether your relationship with them is balanced. Look at the dynamics with your family members, friends, coworkers, or significant other. Are you giving and receiving equally? Are you usually frustrated or happy with them and their behaviors?

Members of your Soul Family may occupy different roles in your life. You might notice that you share intellectual conversations with some friends and family members. With others, you share a good time. With others, if you are lucky, you engage on a number of levels and a variety of interests, especially what is important to you. While different members of your Soul Family balance different aspects of you, they share the ability to give and receive love equally with you.

To create your Soul Family, let's proceed with the following goals.

1. Release your expectations.
2. Want without expectations.
3. Manifest a Soul Family.

Goal 1: *Release your expectations.*

If you look closely at your relationships, you might discover that sometimes you see people not for what they are but for what you want them to be and—actually more often—what you *need* them to be. When the other person does not comply with what are essentially your imagined expectations of him or her, you feel hurt, angry, or disappointed.

Of course, we all have expectations of one another to some degree. You expect that the waiter at a restaurant will serve you; that a dentist will work on your teeth; that your mother will love you; and that your friend will want to go to a movie with you.

However, false expectations—not seeing a person for who he or she really is apart from the role he or she plays—have the unwelcome side effect of putting you into your Fear Response. You are not seeing this person's true qualities. Rather, you are hoping he or she will fulfill the qualities you lack in yourself. This is a setup for disillusionment and dissatisfaction with the relationship and an invitation to the Fear Response to come right in.

I am not telling you not to have expectations, just as I haven't told you not to have fear. Expectations, like negative emotions, are hardwired into you. They exist to signal you that you are unhappy or that something is out of balance within you or around you. Expectations are an indicator that your Fear Response is active. The problem arises when you cannot separate yourself from your expectations and you become angry and upset when they are not met, causing you to behave hurtfully to yourself or others.

Your expectations reflect a distorted representation of your deeper needs. As you have discovered, most people are not aware of what these needs or fears are. Like negative emotions, your expectations are products of your Fear Response, acting as clues that will guide you to dig deeper into your wounds. As you dig, you will uncover what your true needs actually are so that you can take care of them once and for all and no longer expect someone else to do it for you.

You can then feel more whole and complete, and, as a result, you will have fewer expectations of others. You may want them to do or be certain things, but you won't expect it of them. You can make rational decisions about each relationship, see and appreciate the person for his or her true nature, and better handle any strife. You will know whether your love is balanced with this person and if you are giving and receiving equally.

HAZEL: *Transforming Expectations*

Hazel was forty-eight years old, married for twenty-two years, and had two teenage boys. When she came to see me, she was entering menopause and complaining of hot flashes and insomnia. She said that she was crying constantly and needed to get her emotions under control. She also wanted to get control over her two teenage boys, who were having problems in school and fighting with their father incessantly. She was upset that her husband did not connect with anyone, unless it was through sports. None of them ever listened to her or helped around the house, especially her husband. It was a constant battle to try to keep everything under control.

I asked Hazel, "Are you good at taking or asking for help?" "Not so good," she admitted. "And why," I added, "do you have a need for everything to be under control?" "I am a control freak?" she guessed. "I'll get back to you on that," I said encouragingly.

I asked her about her childhood. Hazel had been born to immigrant parents who worked very hard to make a life for their four children. Her father was Italian, tense and emotional. Hazel was the "apple of his eye." Unfortunately, he was rarely home, as he worked so much. Her mother, on the other hand, stayed at home but was not very affectionate and rarely displayed emotion. Hazel described her older siblings as "pretty wild," especially her oldest sister, who was then known as the "black sheep" of the family. Hazel, on the other hand, was the "good girl." She did well in school, was very independent, had many friends, rarely needed help, and rarely added to the drama of the family. She was reliable and responsible. She was a girl who was "always in control."

I went on to ask Hazel what kind of emotions she was experiencing that made her feel out of control. She said she felt really angry at her family for never listening and not behaving the way she thought they should, especially her husband. I also asked Hazel if she wanted to leave her husband. She adamantly answered, "No."

"What do you want, then?" I asked. "You are angry and unhappy, but you do not want to leave. What do you want?"

Hazel quickly replied, "I want him to be kinder, more caring."

"Has he ever behaved in this way?" I inquired.

"No, not really," she admitted.

"So what about his behavior surprises you after twenty-two years? Why do you expect him to be different?" I questioned further. "You want your husband to be something he is not and may never be. You cannot control other people's behavior."

From this conversation, Hazel realized that her desire to control her world was leading her to set up expectations that were not being met and causing her to be angry. I explained to her that the need to be in control stems from fear of the future and lack of trust that all would be well. She would have to heal her fear and learn how to feel whole and complete.

As a remedy, I taught Hazel to create the SHIELD, fill her heart with compassion and acceptance, and repeat the Heart Prayer. I then asked her to create a "want list."

I explained that most people know what they don't want but very few people know what they do want. When people spend much of their time complaining about what they hate or are unhappy about, they trigger the Fear Response. So not only are they miserable, but they activate a negative physiology, which ultimately hurts them, not to mention generates more negative emotions and attitudes.

I clarified that by filling herself with love and compassion, she could feel more complete and whole so that she would have fewer expectations. With fewer expectations she could gain clarity as to what was best for her, what she wanted. Hazel was then to communicate her "wants" to her husband and perhaps consider marriage counseling.

Hazel wanted support. She wanted better communication. She wanted her husband to work with her as a unit and help with the boys.

Unfortunately, marriage counseling failed miserably. Her husband complained about his children the entire time, making Hazel angrier.

While Hazel was trying to work through her anger and fear, her marriage was put to a final test when she was diagnosed with breast cancer. She decided to have a total mastectomy, followed by reconstructive breast surgery. Hazel would need all the support she had from friends and extended family to help her through her recovery. I taught her the Love Radar, a visualization in which you call love to you (you'll learn this next).

Hazel was bedridden for some time after the surgery, requiring a lot of care. Though helped by friends and family, her husband was not supportive of her decision to undergo a total mastectomy, nor was he helpful. Rather, he was resentful and acted like a child whose mother was not paying attention to him.

For Hazel, it was the last straw. She understood that she was the "giver" in the relationship and was married to a "taker." The love here was not in balance. Even a threat to her life could not break him out of his pattern. She knew she was not helping herself by staying in a relationship that was not equally giving and receiving.

When Hazel regained her strength and returned to her everyday activities, she filed for divorce. Today she will tell you that she has never felt better or happier as she surrounds herself only with people with whom she shares balanced love. She knows what she wants, and she now trusts that she will get it. She is learning to let go of her need to control, and in the process she feels more in control than ever.

THE LOVE RADAR EXERCISE

The Love Radar is an exercise that helps fill your heart with love and, at the same time, "call out" to the universe so you can attract the love you want and need in your life. The Love Radar involves visualizing a sphere of light that spins and radiates, like the sun, from the center of the chest. These light rays radiate out to the world and universe, transmitting a call for love or whatever it is you want. Imagine that the Love Radar is also bidirectional, so that as you call out for love and help, you receive love through returning rays of light.

TRY IT

The Love Radar looks like a sun shining inside your heart, radiating light rays in all directions as it spins around and around. Keep that image in mind and repeat to yourself:

"CALLING ALL LOVE! CALLING ALL LOVE!"

Do this exercise as often as you want. You can do it very quickly, and the results can be just as quick. Whenever you feel helpless, overwhelmed, or unable to change a situation, or whenever you need anything—whether it is a new job, new relationship, courage, help of any kind—call on your Love Radar and see what happens.

Your Love Rx for Examining and Resetting Expectations

AWARENESS EXERCISE

Part 1: Examining Your Expectations

Set a timer for ten minutes.
Close your eyes.
Inhale deeply.
Exhale completely.
Let go of thoughts from your mind and tension in your body as you exhale.
Create your SHIELD.
Begin to think about one relationship in which you are experiencing some conflict. (It does not need to be a big conflict. It can be small—a disagreement, a difference of opinion, something that frustrates you about this person, etc.)

Allow your negative or judgmental thoughts or feelings
 toward this person to come to mind.
Recognize that you are not bad for feeling or thinking this way.
Reflect on why this person upsets you so much.
 Have this person's actions hurt you in some way?
 Is this person taking too much?
 Are you giving too much without receiving?
Notice how your chest or your heart feels.
Notice how you are breathing as you entertain these thoughts.
Notice how you feel when you recall this person acting in
 this frustrating or hurtful way.
Have you experienced this feeling before in your past?
Is it a familiar feeling?
Ask your heart to show you a time in your past, recent or
 remote, when you also had this feeling. (If you need help
 asking your heart to reveal your inner thoughts and
 feelings to you, use the Heart Awareness exercise that you
 learned near the end of the previous chapter.)
When did you first recall this feeling?
What happened?
How old were you?
How did you feel?
When the timer goes off, stop and open your eyes.

Part 2: The Release

Reset the timer for five minutes, or more if you like.

1. Write about the experience of this exercise without thinking, judging, or repressing any thoughts or feelings. Write until the timer goes off. Do not stop until then. If you have difficulty with this exercise, that is okay. You can begin by simply writing down your feelings toward this person, as you did in the previous chapter on anger. Keep writing. Look back at the questions from time to time so they can guide your stream of thought. Your writing may take you to a time in the past that turns out to be a significant trigger of your current reactions.

2. When the timer goes off, place your hands on the words and

say, "I now release you from my body." Then destroy the paper by tearing or burning it and do Part 3: Filling Yourself with Love Using the Love Radar. If necessary, continue doing this exercise for the next three to seven days until you feel you have fully released your anger, always ending the session with the Love Radar.

Part 3: The Healing: Filling Yourself with Love Using the Love Radar

This is an expanded version of the abbreviated Love Radar exercise you did earlier.

Close your eyes.
Inhale deeply.
Exhale completely.
Let go of thoughts from your mind and any tension in your body as you exhale.
Create your SHIELD with your divine parents holding you and comforting you.
The divine light fills your heart with compassion and love.
The divine light accumulates in your heart center until it starts forming a ball of light.
The ball of light is like the sun, so as the light accumulates in your heart center, you have a sun shining in the center of your heart.
The sun in the center of your heart begins to revolve and spin.
Rays of divine light shine out from the sun in the center of your heart, just like the sun in the sky.
Now silently repeat these words: "Calling all love! Calling all love!"
By doing so, you are stimulating your Love Radar.
The rays of light shine out of the sun in the center of your heart, out to the world. Calling all love! Calling all love!
Your Love Radar transmits the call for help.
Your Love Radar brings love into your heart and also transmits love out to the world.
Love in and love out, as you inhale and exhale.

Calling all love! Calling all love!
Now ask for whatever you want:
   Clarity
   Abundance
   Guidance
   The right man for me
   The right woman for me
   The right job for me
   The right solution for the situation for me
You can ask for anything.
Do this for at least twenty cycles.

Daily Reprogramming Tools for Releasing Expectations

WHAT TO DO

- Create the SHIELD with the divine parents holding you and comforting you.
- Imagine the divine light shining down on you and filling your heart with compassion and love as you repeat the Heart Prayer:

THE HEART PRAYER
   May my heart receive the light today.
   May my heart be open to love.
   May the light touch my heart today
   And open my heart to love.

- Say the positive verbal command "I trust that I am loved and supported and that I am worthy of receiving love."
- As the light accumulates in your heart, initiate your Love Radar.
- Practice visualizing receiving love from your close family and friends; practice saying "Yes" to help.
- Practice saying "No" when you give at your own expense and it causes you to feel resentful.
- Keep asking yourself, before and after you do the SHIELD, "What do I want, and what is right for me?"
- Create a "want list" to help you gain clarity and manifest your heart's desire.

Use the want list specifically for improving your relationships, but you can also use it to attract whatever you need or desire.

- Find a sheet of paper and create two columns.
- One column will read "Don't Wants" and the other column will read "Wants."
- You can create different categories for career, romance, family, hobby, etc.—anything that you want to create or have in your life.
- Initially, you may not know what you want, so instead, write down what you don't want and then, in your "want" section, write down the opposite of what you wrote for the "don't want." For instance, you know that you do not want a partner who is sullen or emotionally withdrawn. On the "want" side you can write, "Someone with a happy disposition." Or "Someone who can share feelings." You can also start generically with a statement such as "I want the perfect man for me" or "I want the perfect job for me." The important thing is simply to start the list.
- Add to your want list as often as you like, getting more and more detailed and specific as you go along and learn to want without expectations.

- Set a time every day to read your want list. Do this after you do your SHIELD or after you elicit the relaxation response, when awakening in the morning or before going to bed at night.
- Anytime during your day, feel free to add to your list and become more specific with your wants.

WHEN TO USE THE REPROGRAMMING TOOLS
- When you feel your needs or wants are not being met.
- When you feel lonely even when you are not alone.
- When you feel guilty about doing or not doing something.
- When you use the word "should" on yourself—"I should do this" or "I should have done that."
- When you feel you are not deserving of receiving something, even a compliment.
- When you feel attacked.
- When you feel like attacking.
- When you feel disappointed.
- When your heart feels as if it has been broken.

Goal 2. Want without expectations.

CHANGING YOUR BELIEFS AND ASSUMPTIONS

Many of you do not have a support network or financial security. You may not feel you can safely leave your marriages or your jobs. Not everyone has a loyal family or other necessary resources readily available. Leaving your situation is simply not an option right now. What happens then?

The same reprogramming tools apply to you, perhaps even more so, since your Fear Response is further stirred by your feelings of being trapped or made helpless by your circumstance. You will have to consciously fill yourself and your life with love and compassion and slowly build a support network before you can make a life-changing move.

 JEFF: *Changing His Attitude Instead of His Situation*

At age sixty-four, Jeff came to me complaining of chronic chest pain that had followed a traumatic procedure on his heart. He described how he had gone into cardiac arrest during the procedure and that his chest had to be cracked open so that emergency bypass surgery could be performed. He had a long recovery that was made more grueling since his wife offered little support at the time. In addition to the chronic chest pain, Jeff complained of recurrent nightmares, insomnia, and uncontrollable bouts of anger.

As I got to know Jeff, I learned that he had also had a difficult childhood in which he had been abused. As a teenager and young adult, he turned to alcohol, drugs, and the "fast life." He made a lot of money and spent more. Feeling dissatisfied, he began looking for help and turned to spirituality, finding solace in the practice of Buddhism. He got married and had two children.

He was, however, unhappy in his marriage. He was angry that his wife did not support him in any way emotionally, let alone physically. She smoked in the house, despite his asking her not to because it worsened his condition. She never accompanied him to the doctor. She never asked how he was doing. She acted as if she didn't care. It hurt. It reminded him of his childhood. He simply could not trust her to support him in times of need.

I worked with Jeff over several sessions addressing his fears re-
garding safety and concerns about his own physical survival or
death. I had to help him reprogram the experience of trust. First and
foremost, we worked on his developing trust with a medical person
(that would be me!). We also addressed issues of self-worth and his
ability to connect and to receive love, especially from the few friends
or family that he was close to.

Much of our work involved using the SHIELD, the healing visualizations of receiving love and support, and repeating the Trust and
Heart Prayers and the positive verbal command "I trust that I am
loved and supported and worthy of receiving love."

We worked with his anger and with his need to overpower and
control those around him by addressing his lack of self-worth. He
learned to fill his heart with loving kindness and compassion. I asked
Jeff to create his SHIELD, especially anytime he felt he might lash out
in anger or frustration. I asked him to try to take the time to breathe
and reflect before reacting, then choose the appropriate words to express himself.

Working on Jeff's heart was difficult, as he experienced more
chest pain when we addressed his issues. We gently worked through
past hurts and traumas, especially in childhood, which helped him
see that his anger toward others stemmed from his resentment
toward his parents. At the root of his expectations was a need for unconditional parental love. As a remedy, I taught him the Parental
Love Healing.

I guided Jeff to visualize himself back in his childhood being surrounded by the SHIELD with the divine parents, receiving abundant
love and affection, repeating the Trust Prayer and his positive verbal
command. I instructed him to practice this reprogramming tool as
often as possible.

Jeff found that he felt calmer and more at peace and was angry
less often. He began to widen his social circle. He volunteered at a
local senior center, joined a political campaign, and started taking
daily walks with his cousin Fred. In the meantime, Jeff's wife agreed
to smoke outside the house and actually asked him how he was doing
after he returned from his visit with me. Husband and wife were
slowly becoming civil to each other. As time went on, Jeff realized
that his relationship with his wife was not "ideal" but was more of a
friendship than anything else.

Jeff also knew that he would never leave his wife. It simply was
not an option. Therefore, his only recourse was to work on himself,

work on developing a circle of friends and family that could offer more of the love and support that he needed, and continue to work on his old wounds surrounding feelings of abandonment and rejection.

Your Love Rx for Changing Your Negative Beliefs

AWARENESS EXERCISE

Part 1. Do the same Awareness Exercise as you did in Goal 1 (pp. 100–103).

Part 2. Do the same Release Exercise as you did in Goal 1 (p. 101).

Every time you do these exercises, different realizations and insights will come, taking you to a new level of healing.

Then do the healing exercise below.

Part 3: The Healing: Receiving Unconditional Love and Support

Close your eyes.
Inhale deeply.
Exhale completely.
Let go of thoughts from your mind and tension in your body
    as you exhale.
Create your SHIELD.
Imagine a divine mother and father are standing in your
    SHIELD of light.
They are repeating the Trust Prayer, and they hold you and
    comfort you:
    Trust.
    Trust that you are not alone.
    Trust that you did nothing wrong.
    Trust that you are loved and lovable.
    That you are the expression of a divine energy
    And perfect just as you are.
Allow yourself to be rocked, cradled, nurtured, and held.

Relax into their love.

The divine light from the SHIELD melts into your heart, filling your heart with compassion and love.

Say these words: "I trust that I am loved and supported and that I am worthy of receiving love."

Inhale as the light fills your heart with compassion and love.

Exhale as the light spreads throughout your chest.

Say these words: "I trust that I am loved and supported and that I am worthy of receiving love."

Retrieve the image of yourself from your awareness exercise—the image of yourself in the past feeling hurt, afraid, or somehow bad.

Imagine you are embracing the old image of yourself.

Tell the old image of yourself to:

Trust.

Trust that you are not alone.

Trust that you did nothing wrong.

Trust that you are loved and lovable,

That you are the expression of a divine energy

And perfect just as you are.

Feel the old image of yourself relaxing into your arms as you hold her/him and comfort her/him.

The old image of yourself will begin saying these words: "I trust that I am loved and supported and that I am worthy of receiving love" as you hold her/him.

The SHIELD of divine light will surround you both and melt into your hearts.

The divine parents still stand by your side, comforting and holding you both.

You are both feeling more at peace, more whole, more confident.

Your old image merges into your image.

You are feeling more at peace, more whole and confident.

You are feeling more accepting of yourself and your situation.

Daily Reprogramming Tools for Receiving Unconditional Love and Support

WHAT TO DO

- Create your SHIELD with your divine parents holding you and comforting you, repeating the Trust Prayer.
- Imagine the divine light is filling your heart.
- Bring up the old image of yourself and comfort that image.
- Say the positive verbal command "I trust that I am loved and supported and that I am worthy of receiving love."
- Practice asking for help.
- Find a therapist or doctor with whom you can connect. If you do not like that person, leave and look elsewhere.
- Begin to create a support network. Join a support group, community program, church, synagogue, etc. You can even join a book club or other club that shares your interests.
- Just take notice when you feel your expectations are not being met and ask yourself to be more clear about what those expectations or needs really are.
- Add to your "Want List" as you gain more clarity of your needs, what you can compromise and what you cannot.

WHEN TO USE THE REPROGRAMMING TOOLS

- When you feel let down by a friend, family, partner, boss, colleague, etc.
- When you feel you have let someone else down.
- When you feel frustrated, resentful, or angry toward someone.
- When you have made someone else resentful, angry, or frustrated.
- When you feel anxious, needy, or desperate (i.e. waiting for the phone to ring).

Goal 3: Manifest a Soul Family.

Relationships require communication. It is one thing to work through your fears and expectations, another to translate your wants and feelings to another person and, in turn, understand their true wants and feelings.

• When you examine your relationships, you look at whether you are satisfied or dissatisfied, and you pinpoint your unmet expectations. You then peer deeper into these unmet expectations to discover their origin or the underlying wound from your past that you now have some prescriptions to remedy. As you heal, you find yourself more at peace and better capable of making decisions about your circumstances.

However, this isn't enough. In order to have a relationship, you have to interact and communicate with another person. Ridding yourself of expectations means nothing if the two of you do not communicate with each other, about each other's wants and desires. We expect people to read our minds. On the other side of that coin, you cannot read their minds. When there is flow in a two-way communication, there is balance in the circle. It is really so much easier to communicate when you have clarity as to what your wants are in the first place.

It is also more effortless to attract and unite with the people who complete your balanced circle of love. That sense of flow is how you know they are part of your Soul Family.

 MY EXAMPLE: *Clarifying and Communicating Your Needs*

Believe me, I've had my share of imbalanced relationships! For as long as I can think back, my choice has been to withdraw from people whom I believed had hurt me. If and when I felt mistreated, I would close myself off from that person and walk away from the situation without trying to talk, mostly because I was too scared to use my voice. I did finally learn my lesson with my friend John.

John had ended a long relationship shortly before I met him. He was depressed, and we spent hours talking about his depression, whether we were out for dinner, having a drink, at the beach, or hiking in the mountains. I was happy to counsel and support. I needed to be needed, and John needed support. Initially, the relationship served us both. However, when I started having my own difficult experiences, I also needed support and care. John could not do that for me. He was still wrapped up in his own problems. I reverted to my Fear Response, feeling hurt and disappointed. I felt resentful and angry, believing that I had given so much and was not receiving in return. I felt angry with him for not noticing that I was not my usual smiling self. I distanced myself from John rather than speaking to him about my feelings.

Distancing myself allowed me to look inward and reflect on what I truly needed. I used my SHIELD, asked for help, embraced myself as a hurt little girl, and found friends and family to support me. As I became stronger, I began to gain some clarity. I realized that the little girl in me was hurt by John's actions and that I had reacted by distancing myself because of my Fear Response. But by distancing myself, I had abandoned our friendship and him. I had hurt him.

By the time I tried to reconnect with John, he was very angry with me. His e-mails to me were filled with hurt and angry accusations, which I initially reacted to with my own anger, hurt, and resentment. I knew we would have to meet and talk about it. But initially I resisted. At first I was apprehensive, worried about what he might say, and how I might react. I reflected, "If I were to act out of my highest good, what would I do?" I created my SHIELD and visualized embracing my little girl. I then visualized my divine parents embracing both of us and repeated the Trust Prayer. I also gave myself what I needed—a hug.

As I hugged myself and repeated my positive verbal command, I immediately shifted out of my Fear Response. The negative feelings were soon replaced by feelings of graciousness and love, so that I was able to forgive us both. I picked up the phone and said I was sorry and that I wanted to meet.

I could hear in his voice that he was pleased, and I knew I was doing the right thing. I had taken care of myself and acted in this relationship, as in any other relationship, from a place of love, rather than from a place of fear or anger. My job was to know that I was not perfect and that my behavior had been less than perfect. That instead of talking about my hurt with my friend, I had closed myself off and turned away. I didn't trust the friendship, and I was wrong this time. John was very giving in many ways; I just had to ask for what I needed. And what he said when we did meet woke me up to my misjudgment. He said that he might be clueless, but he was a loyal friend. He is indeed a member of my Soul Family now that we've figured out how to give and take love in a balanced way.

Your Love Rx for Manifesting Your Soul Family

AWARENESS EXERCISE

Part 1: Awareness About Current Family Expectations

> Set a timer for ten minutes.
> Close your eyes.
> Inhale deeply.
> Exhale completely.
> Let go of thoughts from your mind and tension in your body as you exhale.
> Create your SHIELD.
> Begin to think about your family as they are now.
> Think about the dynamics in your family and how your family members perceive you.
> Notice passing thoughts and emotions as if you are watching a movie. Just notice.
> Allow your thoughts and images to take you back in time, as if you are watching a movie of your family life and you are viewing different scenes.
> See yourself as a child, infant, or young adult.
> Notice the dynamics.
> Notice your role.
> Notice how you felt you were perceived.
> Allow your thoughts, images, and emotions to come up, without trying to change anything, repress it, or judge it.
> When the timer goes off, stop and open your eyes.

Part 2: The Release of Negative Feelings About Family

Reset the timer for fifteen minutes.

1. You can talk to a friend or write about your experience and what you feel. The point of this release is to let go of your expectations of what you think a family should be. But first you need to see what your expectations are and what led you to feel the way you do. By letting go of your past, you are releasing

old patterns and behaviors that set in through your life with your family.

2. When the timer goes off, place your hands on the words and say, "I now release you from my body," and destroy the paper. If you are telling a friend about your experience, when you are done, say these words out loud or just say to yourself: "I now have released you from my body."

Part 3: Healing: The Soul Family

This healing visualization keys off the Love Radar exercise, with the addition of the call out for your Soul Family. You can request to attract a specific person or make a general call out to your Soul Family.

Close your eyes.
Inhale deeply.
Exhale completely.
Let go of thoughts from your mind and tension in your body
    as you exhale.
Create your SHIELD with your divine parents holding you
    and comforting you.
Imagine that a divine light is filling your heart with
    compassion and love and is accumulating in your heart
    center.
As the light accumulates in your heart center, it starts
    forming a sun.
The sun is shining out from the center of your heart as it
    spins and revolves.
Initiate your Love Radar.
Repeat these words silently: "Calling all love! Calling all
    love!"
The rays of light will shine out of your heart center, out to
    the world. Calling all love! Calling all love!
Keep calling out for love, and the radar will keep
    transmitting the call for help.
At the same time, as the radar is coming from your heart, it
    will be transmitting love out to the world.
Now ask for your Soul Family to appear in your life.
Ask for your life partner.

For a best friend.
For someone to mother you.
For someone whom you can mother.
For your work partners.
And so on.
Ask for your Soul Family to come into your life.

Daily Reprogramming Tools for Manifesting a Soul Family

WHAT TO DO

- Practice asking for help, even if it is just when you are doing your SHIELD and asking no one in particular. This action is programming the habit of surrendering and allowing yourself to receive love and support in whichever form it comes in.
- Set an intention to connect with a friend or loved one at least once a day—either by phone or in person.
- Find a "phone buddy": You and a friend or loved one make a commitment to speak on the phone for as long as you have time for—ten to sixty minutes—once a week. Make set dates on your calendar for at least six months out. This way, you always know that at least once a week, you will have the opportunity to open up to someone, to give and receive love.
- The mother's touch: Experience healing touch with energy healing, massage, or craniosacral therapy, relaxing baths, and lots of hugs! (I have been known to chase my patients down the street if they have left my office without a hug!) This is another way of reprogramming the act of receiving into your subconscious.
- The Soul Family pet: If you can, get yourself a pet or spend some quality time with someone else's pet. Pets are wonderful sources of unconditional love and, as studies show, great for your health!
- Practice breath work to remind yourself what the experience of wholeness, of taking in and letting go, feels like. You can always practice the Love Circle breath exercise that you learned earlier:

Sit in a comfortable position.
Focus on the inhalation.
Breathe in deeply.

Focus on the exhalation.

Exhale completely.

Notice how much air you can take in before you feel as if
   you are going to explode.

Notice how easily you let it go.

Notice how you cannot hold on to your breath even if
   you try.

Notice how when you exhale completely, your inhalation
   begins immediately.

Notice that there is no way to stop the cycle.

Notice how every time you let go of your breath, a new
   breath of life comes in.

Focus on your chest as the breath moves in and out.

Breathe in life.

Let go, sharing it with the world.

Breathe in love.

Let go, sharing it with the world.

Do this for at least ten cycles.

WHEN TO USE THE REPROGRAMMING TOOLS

- When you feel lonely.
- When you feel you do not have anyone to talk to.
- When you feel dissatisfied with your home or work life.
- When you notice you have too many imbalanced relationships.
- When you notice that most of your friends are takers, not
  givers.
- When you crave connection.

Allowing yourself to receive love is the best method for learning
how to love yourself. As in the Breath Circle—when you experience
breathing fully and completely—you notice how much better it feels
compared to holding your breath or breathing shallowly. You say to
yourself, "Hey, that doesn't feel so good and I want to feel good. I deserve it. I want to take longer and deeper breaths!" The same goes for
the Love Circle. The more you receive and give love equally with others, the more you understand what feels good to you and you deserve
it. You learn that you indeed are worthy of receiving love, which ultimately prepares you to learn Self-Love.

8

THE LOVE PYRAMID

Building Self-Love

The Self-Love section of the Love Pyramid originates in one main principle: each and every one of us is unique and great.

If you are like many of my patients, you are reading that last line and thinking "If I am so unique and great, why do I feel like crap?"

Self-Love is often the most difficult form of love to achieve. It is a challenge to feel good about yourself and love yourself when you are in the Fear Response. You tend to forgo exercise, eat poorly, eat too much or too little, or lack sufficient sleep—all of which makes you feel even worse.

When you feel miserable, you are usually no joy to be around, so others tend to avoid you. Therefore you feel lonely and unlovable, reinforcing the downward spiral.

When you lack Self-Love, you feel somehow incomplete and unwhole. You believe that you are good enough only if something or someone else completes you. You assume that the structure and security of your life depend on externals—your job, your education, your standing in the community, your financial status, even your family. If or when those external factors are jeopardized, your very existence becomes unstable and nebulous. You may feel helpless or uncertain, less sure of who you are and how to live. You may waver in your faith and purpose in life. Obsessed with your losses, you become lost to yourself and unable to find your way out of the Fear Response.

However, when you possess Self-Love, the opposite occurs. You feel more centered and less impacted by negative things. You accept your imperfections as part of your individual makeup and conditioning, neither good nor bad. You know who you are. You break free of the barriers you have created and have the courage and strength to move smoothly through life's obstacles. And, yes, you recognize yourself as unique and great.

LEARNING TO LOVE YOURSELF

Developing Self-Love means learning to perceive yourself without judgment. It also means practicing self-nurturance. Just as affection flows from Social Love, self-nurturance is the action that results from Self-Love. Self-nurturance involves taking care of your body with good nutrition and habits; paying attention to your physical and emotional needs; treating yourself the way you would treat someone you love. When you do this, you are open, relaxed, and receptive. You explore and discover who you are and who you are meant to become. You develop the support to build self-confidence and self-esteem and accept yourself just the way you are.

Self-Love is not an option. It is a necessity. People who base their own self-worth on what others think often pay a mental and physical price, according to research by Jennifer Crocker, Ph.D., a psychologist at the University of Michigan's Institute for Social Research.

Crocker surveyed 642 college freshmen, having them fill out a questionnaire that assessed their overall level of self-esteem and their endorsement of both external and internal foundations of self-esteem, including competition, appearance, approval of others, family support, virtue, religious faith, and competence. The initial survey, given before they left for college, revealed that overall the students had a high level of self-esteem. More than 80 percent of the students said they based their self-worth on academic competence, 77 percent on their family's support, 66 percent on doing better than others, 65 to 70 percent on their appearance, 66 percent on being a good person, 40 percent on religious faith, and 37 percent on the approval of others.

At the end of the fall and spring terms, the researchers followed up their survey with an assessment of how the freshmen were faring socially and academically. Crocker found that college students who based their self-worth on external sources—including appearance, approval from others, and their academic performance—reported more stress, anger, academic problems, and relationship conflicts. They also had higher levels of drug and alcohol use and symptoms of eating disorders.

Students who based their self-esteem on internal sources—such as being a virtuous person or adhering to moral standards—earned higher grades and were less likely to use alcohol and drugs or to develop eating disorders.[1]

For me, the path to discovering my true self was frightening at first. I feared that I would not like what I saw. I was not ready to truly accept myself without judgment. It took a lot of convincing for me to love myself and all of my imperfections. But it grew easier and easier as I realized my worth and value as a human being, imperfections and all. I found that when I felt anxious or angry or insecure, I did not feel "right." When I *did* feel "right"—or "centered," as some people say—it felt as if I had stepped into myself, into the person I truly was and was always meant to be. The more centered I felt, the more I followed my passions and worried less about what others thought or expected of me. By accepting myself without judgment, I was better able to discern my reason for being here on this earth. I knew that if I simply followed my own path, I would receive happiness, love, health, friendships, and everything else I value in life. Most important, I would be better able to buffer my Fear Response, which in turn helped me feel increasingly better about myself.

REPEAT AFTER ME

You can strengthen your Self-Love with the repetition of this simple but powerful positive verbal command:

"I am loved."

Repeat these words often, and you may find that you feel more loved and lovable and healthier altogether. It works. With repetition of this positive verbal command, you are replacing the negative assumptions of "I am not loved," "I am bad," "I am being punished" with the positive belief of being loved, no matter what. In doing so, you reprogram your physiology from ongoing Fear Response to Love Response activation.

THE ORIGINS OF YOUR SENSE OF SELF

Not surprisingly, Self-Love starts in early childhood. When you experience parental bonding and affection, pleasant sensations, positive rewards, and increased neural pathway formation as a child, you develop the belief and attitude that you can handle life's challenges. You believe that you are worthy and capable of receiving love and support. You recognize that you have resources such as family and friends (Social Love) and assume that you deserve access to them. You develop a better sense of control. Research supports the assumption that expectations and beliefs can affect physiological responses and that individuals with a stronger sense of control are healthier,[2] as their Fear Response stays dormant more often.

With self-confidence and a sense of control, you believe you are able to influence outcomes. You choose more adaptive behaviors rather than go into the Fear Response. You feel less shame because you feel you have less to hide. Research shows that people with more feelings of shame tend to be happy less often[3] and associate even positive life events with poor health.[4] In contrast, people with higher self-esteem tend to be happier and associate positive life events with good health.[5]

Note that a strong sense of self is associated *not* with fearlessness but with the willingness and ability to approach a challenge despite the fact that it is fear-provoking. This trait is courage, a word rooted in the Latin word for *heart*. When you have courage, you feel you can conquer your fear and meet challenges because your heart is full of self-confidence.

The more negative conditioning you have experienced, the less likely you will feel supported, loved, and capable of handling your fears, and the more damaged and empty your heart becomes. Deep within your heart rests the emotional memories that fuel your negative beliefs and assumptions that form the basis of your self-image and self-worth.

So what happens if your early childhood and early experiences were negative, fear-inducing, and unsupported? Are you doomed?

Quite the contrary. When you learn to give and receive love from others and the world around you, you are more able to reach into the deep place within you where beliefs can change into viewpoints that support and nourish your life. You can then literally reprogram yourself into self-esteem.

PETER: *Shame*

Peter was fifty-six years old when he walked into my office, complaining of lacking self-confidence and energy. He was tired all the time, which did not prevent him from doing his work or other daily activities, but nonetheless the feeling of tiredness was always there. He felt he had low mental energy as well as low physical energy. He said he slept well and had no other problems, aside from neck and upper-back tension, which seemed to have existed for as long as he could recall.

Peter was self-employed, and he did well in his business. He was married and had no children. He did not feel stressed from his workload and reported having a good relationship with his wife. He said he was a vegetarian and ate a healthy diet. He took vitamins, exercised, and meditated regularly. He strongly believed in a higher power and felt this belief got him through the difficulties in his life.

On first view, it seemed that Peter had adequate social support as well as a sense of spiritual connection. Yet he still felt tired, had muscle tension, and had low self-confidence, meaning to me that he lacked self-love. On further questioning, Peter told me about his childhood.

Peter's father had died at the time of his younger brother's birth. His mother had then abandoned him and his younger brother to an orphanage when he was three years old. Peter had lived there until he turned thirteen. He described life at the orphanage as being similar to what you see in the movies—very strict, unemotional, and unnurturing. Since both he and his brother were small in size, he needed to be strong to fight and protect himself and his brother from the bullies. He recalled that at one point he was up for adoption but refused to separate from his brother, wishing to stay with him. By the time he was thirteen, he was able to leave the orphanage and go into foster homes. He and his brother then moved from one home to the next, sometimes receiving nurturing care and other times receiving abusive or negligent care. Peter started working at age sixteen and, while continuing his education, supported himself and his younger brother.

Essentially, Peter had been abandoned. His early childhood development did not include parental love and nurturance and the belief that he was wanted, loved, and cared for. As a result, his ability to develop self-confidence and a strong sense of self-worth was diminished.

Peter's tasks therefore involved working on his image of self, his sense of worth, and his ability to receive the love and support that was around him. Through use of positive verbal commands and self-suggestion exercises, Peter slowly overrode his ingrained feelings of shame and low self-confidence. In time, as his physiology improved, his energy level rose and his muscle pain went away.

Spend a moment reflecting on these questions:

- When you walk into a room full of strangers whom you may need to impress, do you feel comfortable or insecure?
- Do you worry about the way you look or sound?
- Do you project confidence when you speak?
- How much do you depend on their approval?
- How do you react when someone questions or criticizes your ideas, projects, or work?
- If someone questions or criticizes you, do you speak up for yourself and your values?
- Do you react with anger, or do you clam up and say nothing at all?

When you have Self-Love, you have confidence, even among strangers and in stressful situations. You do not depend on others for approval or validation. You handle criticism because you do not take it personally, and you express yourself clearly.

How can you get to this place of confidence and clarity?

By becoming whole.

BEING WHOLE

Try this exercise: Draw a big circle, as if you are drawing a picture of a pie. The pie represents your life, so slice it up into sections. Each slice represents something that is important to you, such as family, friends, work, etc. You also want to include slices reflecting things you want to have but have not acquired yet; things that you believe would "complete you" if you had them.

Most people believe that being whole involves having all of the slices of the pie in place. Otherwise, they feel that, like the pie, they are incomplete and the empty space begs to be filled. They feel insecure and, perhaps, unworthy without that particular slice.

This occurs because most people base their self-image and self-confidence on what they have and do and on the approval or validation of others. The underlying assumption is "I am not enough nor do I have enough."

So how can you change this underlying assumption and learn to become whole?

You can fill yourself up with something else (and I do not mean food, alcohol, or medication). This something is love.

YOUR LOVE CUSHION

Picture this: When you were born, your parents opened a bank account for you. In this account, they deposited all sorts of funds—your nutrition, education, college tuition, a variety of skill sets, and so on. As you grew, other people made deposits into your account as well. The funds you accumulated went into a "reserve" account, meant to help you survive and live in the world.

While you accumulated this knowledge and experience in your fund, you also received deposits of unconditional love. These are your Love Reserves. This account consists of the pure unconditional love you have amassed from others, from Spirit, for just being alive. You do not have to pay back your Love Reserves. There are no strings, no attachments. No one asks anything in return. You exist, therefore you can draw on them when you are in stress or fear. When your account maintains a positive balance, you feel good about yourself.

It is rare, however, to keep a positive balance in your Love Reserves account, simply because life is so stressful and you often have to dip into your funds. You also may not have received sufficient deposits in your Love Reserves in your early life. You may have experienced challenges that have caused you to question who you are supposed to become, who you really are, whether you are loved or lovable or worthy and supported. By the time you are an adult, your Love Reserves may be pretty thin.

BACK TO CHILDHOOD!

The amount of love, nurturance, and acceptance you received in your life, especially early on, established the core of your self-image. Being nurtured and loved in your early years helps you learn that you are valued and valuable. As a newborn, you likely received unconditional love and a big deposit in your Love Reserves. No one had any expectations of you. You were important and loved simply because you existed! Soon others began to form expectations of you. Societal and familial obligations and rules started to influence you. You learned that if you behaved as expected, you gained reward and acknowledgement. A deposit of "conditional love" went into a different "account"—not your Love Reserves, which contains only unconditional love, but a "conditional love" account, which accumulates assets based on your acceptable behavior.

Your early self-image is, then, based on the premise "I am good if I obey and bad if I do not. When I am good, my account grows. When I am bad, my account is depleted." Fewer funds, more fear.

As an adult, the same premise holds. Your Fear Response activates when you do not feel validated or valued. The Fear Response then exacerbates the problem by triggering a hidden wound from an earlier time when you felt the same way. Even if you were raised in a loving environment, a threat to your self-image can set off your Fear Response. No one receives unlimited, unconditional love.

But it is possible for everyone to grow their Love Reserves and Self-Love. It just takes conscious and deliberate awareness and action to make the change. The next chapter will show you how.

9

SELF-LOVE

The Basics for Building Your Love Reserves

C an you relate to this scenario?

Your alarm clock fails to go off, and you oversleep. No time for a shower, breakfast, or coffee; you quickly dress, barely brush your teeth, and rush out of the house only to find yourself stuck in traffic. Arriving late to work, your "bad day" has only just begun. The Diet Coke you picked up from the vending machine explodes all over your shirt. Your computer jams and you have rebooted twice, only to find, when you do get into your e-mail, that your boss has sent you a notice that a big project deadline is now two weeks earlier than before. By the time your friend and colleague stops by to tell you about her date last night, you have no patience. You dismiss her, telling her you have no time for idle chitchat. Offended, she steers clear of you for the rest of the day. Starving, frustrated, and dirty, you go to the office kitchen, where you see a box full of donuts. You scarf down four of them. Now you have gone from being rushed and late to feeling fat and sick and without a best friend.

Now, what if you had a big reserve or cushion of love for your-self? During times of stress, you could pull Self-Love from this reserve—which is like taking out money from your savings account when your checking account is running low. Despite the difficult times, you could maintain self-care behaviors, stay strong and flexi-ble, handle your stress, stimulate the Fear Response less often and less intensely, and generally feel better. In the same scenario, you might choose a shower over arriving at the office exactly on time; find that you actually do have a few minutes to talk to your friend; and discover that you don't actually need those four donuts.

The larger your Love Reserves, the more whole you become, the more confident you are, and the stronger your Self-Love.

Knowing this, your mission is to build up the Self-Love side of your Love Pyramid by meeting the following three goals:

1. Learn to appreciate yourself and know your perfection.
2. Understand how to be free of neediness and attachment.
3. Overcome addictions, shame, and low self-worth.

Goal 1: Learn to appreciate yourself and know your perfection.

To fully appreciate yourself, you have to come to terms with the parts you don't like, and understand why you don't like them. Then you can take a deep look at your "imperfections," appreciate them as part of you, and realize that you are worthy even with your imperfections. In fact, they are the very aspects of yourself that make you unique.

Your Love Rx for Appreciating Yourself

AWARENESS EXERCISE: HOW DO YOU SEE OR DEFINE YOURSELF?

Self-Portrait Now

In this exercise, you will draw a self-portrait according to how you believe others see you. You do not have to be a great artist to do this exercise. You can use words around the picture, perhaps adding arrows to indicate where in your body the words apply. Draw how you think others expect you to be. For instance, you may assume others perceive you as quiet, fun, or reliable; or that they define you by your medical condition, like "the one with breast cancer"; or by your role as a mother, an accountant, etc. You can write these descriptions around the portrait that you draw.

Self-Portrait: Then Versus Now

Now I want you to find a photograph of yourself when you were a child, preferably sometime before age six or seven. If you do not have a photo, close your eyes and see what image of yourself comes up. Either way, study the image. Get to know every detail about this little child. Try to remember what you looked like and felt like at the time. Write words around the image, as you did with the portrait of your current self. Notice how differently you define this young image of yourself as compared to your current self-portrait. Notice which adjectives or descriptions are the same and which are different. Notice how much love or concern you have toward this young image of yourself. Do you feel the same when you look at your current self-portrait?

I ask you to do this exercise because the person who really needs to feel self-worth and self-acceptance is this little child. It was the child part of you that scarfed down the four donuts, even though you knew they were not good for you. Your irrational, not-so-intellectual "child" mind wanted instant relief because he or she felt bad.

It is also easier to love and accept the child part of the self, rather than the adult part. If I were to instruct you to accept yourself and accept your body the way it is now, it might be difficult for you. If you feel fat, telling yourself that you like the way you look is not going to work. In fact, it might make you feel worse. However, you would be far less likely to tell your little self that he or she is ugly and fat. In fact, you would probably say quite the opposite, that he or she looks fabulous. Why hurt this cute and precious child?

The aim of repeatedly complimenting your little self is to reprogram your memory. As your little girl or boy understands her or his worth, your unconscious mind takes it in as fact. Then, when you are in situations that threaten your self-image, your Fear Response is more likely to remain dormant.

Why? Because your Fear Response is not usually set off by your intellectual, rational-thinking mind, which knows better. It is stimulated by unconscious negative assumptions and beliefs you incurred when you were little. By reprogramming your memory, you are effectively reprogramming your unconscious physiology.

HEALING HIDDEN OR OBVIOUS FEELINGS OF SHAME AND LOW SELF-WORTH

Part 1: Awareness of Shame

Set a timer for five minutes.
Close your eyes.
Inhale deeply.
Exhale completely.
Do this several times as you create your SHIELD.
Recall the image of yourself when you were a child.
You wanted to have, be, or to do something and you were not allowed.
Or you had something or loved something or someone, and it was taken away.
Or another child made fun of you for something you had or were.
Or an authority figure did not allow you to cry or get upset and told you to put on a happy face instead.
Take your time and recall the experience.
What happened?
What did you feel?
What do you feel now?
Pay attention to your emotions, your thoughts, the quality of your breathing, the physical sensations you feel in your body, especially in your chest.
When the timer goes off, stop and open your eyes.

Part 2: The Release

Reset the timer for fifteen minutes.

1. Write down your feelings about the above exercise so you can solidify the experience and allow yourself to fully observe and witness what has just occurred. You are now doing "shame release" (like anger release). Let your emotions come through, crying or shouting if you need to.
2. When the timer goes off, stop. As with the anger release journaling, place your hands on the paper and say, "I now release

you from my body." Now shred or burn the paper. Follow this exercise with the Child of Perfection healing below.

Part 3: The Healing: Child of Perfection: Reprogramming to know that you are perfect just as you are

Close your eyes.
Inhale deeply.
Exhale completely.
Let go of negative thoughts, feelings, and energy as you
    exhale. Sweep the negative energy into the earth as you
    exhale.
Create your SHIELD.
Surround yourself with divine light and unconditional love.
Allow the divine light from your SHIELD to fill your heart.
Repeat the Heart Prayer:

THE HEART PRAYER
    May my heart receive the light today.
    May my heart be open to love.
    May the light touch my heart today
    And open my heart to love.

Allow the divine light and love to melt into your heart.
A divine mother hears your prayer and appears in your
    SHIELD.
She rocks and comforts you.
She is proud of you.
She loves you just because you are alive.
She tells you, "You are a child of the universe, created in its
    perfection."
You allow her to cradle, nurture, and hold you.
You say, "I am enough. I have enough."
When you are ready, recall the image of your little child
    feeling hurt or abandoned.
Embrace the little child, hold him or her close to your chest,
    and rock and comfort him or her.
Tell the little child that you are proud of her or him; that
    you love the child just because the child is alive.

Tell the child, "You are a child of the universe, created in its
    perfection."
The little child relaxes into your arms and into your love.
The divine mother wraps her arms around you both,
    creating a SHIELD of divine light and love around both
    of you.
The child begins repeating "I am enough. I have enough."
Do this as long as you wish.
Notice how the demeanor of the little child changes.
Is he or she becoming more confident, secure, playful, more
    loved?

Daily Reprogramming Tools for Self-Worth
The next step is to notice each time your self-worth is in question and
how it triggers your Fear Response.

WHAT TO DO
- Create your SHIELD with a divine mother by your side and
  bring back the image of yourself as a child surrounded by love
  and light. As the divine mother says, "You are a child of the universe, created in its perfection," you say the positive verbal
  command "I am enough. I have enough."
- Repeat the Heart Prayer.
- Do the Love Radar.
- Carry around the picture of yourself as a little child and look at
  it throughout the day. When you do, send love and adoration to
  the child. Imagine telling her or him how magnificent he or she
  is. You may say, "You are a child of the universe, created in its
  perfection." Over time, you will be able to recall the image
  clearly without the need of the photograph.
- Listen to your needs. Ask yourself this question: "If I love myself, would I _____?" For instance, Would I eat this food?
  Would I date this man? Would I not sleep? Would I work so
  hard? Would I ignore this pain in my back?
- Treat yourself with kindness. This means getting a massage,
  buying yourself gifts just because you can, doing things you love
  to do, spending less time doing the things you dislike and being
  around people who hurt you.

- Practice self-care. Listen to your needs and treat yourself with kindness. This involves eating healthfully, exercising, getting plenty of sleep, following up with your doctor and therapist, and getting the help that is right for you.
- Add to your "want list."
- Learn to appreciate yourself by keeping an Appreciation Journal, as described below.

THE APPRECIATION JOURNAL

Every evening, for the next twenty-eight days, write four things about yourself and four things about your life that you appreciate. In the morning, stand in front of the mirror and read the list out loud. Try to come up with new things every day, but if you can't, recycle the previous ones. Many of my patients find this task difficult or tedious, and I would agree, but do it anyway. You are reprogramming old thoughts, beliefs, and attitudes. It gets easier.

WHEN TO USE THE REPROGRAMMING TOOLS

- Anytime you feel bad about yourself.
- When you feel undeserving of something good, even when it is being offered to you.
- When you become upset because you feel your needs have not been met or you simply have not gotten what you wanted.
- Anytime your boss reprimands you, your partner ignores your needs, a man or woman whom you are interested in doesn't pay you the attention you want, or someone yells at you.
- Anytime you blame yourself for something, when you feel you are not good enough or haven't done something well enough.
- Anytime you feel ashamed, whether it is about how you look, where you come from, what you do, or something you have done.
- Anytime you feel intimidated, or low in confidence or self-esteem, such as feeling someone is better than you in one way or another.
- Anytime you feel guilt.

Write in your Appreciation Journal every day.

Goal 2: Understand how to be free of neediness and attachment.

When you feel incomplete or not enough, you attach yourself to people, places, and things. For instance, some of you may believe that having a title—doctor, lawyer, countess, etc.—makes you more important or worthy of respect. Without the title, who would you be? Your attachments and your intensity about those attachments can serve as clues to what needs healing within you.

Although you may have earned many successes, your life has seen its share of failures, losses, and unmet expectations, requiring large withdrawals from your Love Reserves, perhaps even depleting them. This gives way to feelings of loss or emptiness. With this sense of loss has come neediness and attachment to things and people who to you represent success in the areas where you felt failure and loss. Unconsciously, you reach for these people or think that they can replenish your account and help you feel whole and complete.

However, when you do feel whole and complete, you have wants but not needs. You may like certain people or things, but you do not become attached to them. You are not attached to a specific outcome, to whether you succeed or lose, or to whether you need something to happen in a particular way.

 MY STORY: *Attached to My Diamonds*

Several years ago, my father gave my sister and me diamond earrings. I was so thrilled. Not only had I wanted these earrings for as long as I could remember, but I also cherished them because they were a gift from my dad. One day while at work, I noticed that one of the earrings was missing from my ear. I panicked. I searched everywhere—under the carpets, under the desks, under the exam tables. The more I looked, the more upset I became, especially with myself. In my close family and circle of friends, I am well known for losing my material possessions. More than once I have lost my wallet, cameras, and glasses, and, of course, my apartment burned down and I lost everything. I actually prided myself on not having "attachments" to material possessions, as I had learned my lesson time and time again. But this time, I was not so detached. I was really angry at myself for losing this earring and blamed myself for being careless with this cherished gift of love from my father. I felt ashamed and could not face my friends and family, should they find out.

I was also angry. Why did this have to happen to me all the time? Why had I lost that earring, which was so precious to me? I was angry, so I began writing in my journal: "It's not fair. I don't understand. I do everything that I am told. I am a good person. I give to charity. What did I do wrong? What did I do to deserve this? Why am I being punished? I must be a bad person. It is my fault. I should have been paying more attention. I never pay attention. That is why I lose everything all the time. What am I going to tell my family? I am so ashamed."

And then I cried. I simply felt a tremendous sense of loss for losing something so precious, for not feeling good enough, for feeling so unworthy that perhaps I did not deserve to have something so nice and dear.

After writing my feelings down, I destroyed the paper and practiced the Heart Prayer healing. The next day, after work, I went to the jeweler and spent money that I did not have on a replacement earring, begging the salesperson not to tell my father.

The next morning, I sat in meditation, created the SHIELD, and asked my heart to show me why I felt this way. Why did I have so much shame and attachment to these earrings? The image of my little girl self appeared, needing her father's love. In her mind, not receiving his love meant she was somehow a bad person. I understood then that I equated the earrings from my father as a validation of his love. I was in need of love, not earrings—that much became very clear.

As a remedy, I imagined holding my little girl image in my arms, telling her she was perfect as she was, that she was worthy of love, and that her parents loved her. I imagined that she and I were repeating the positive verbal command "I am enough. I have enough." Within minutes, I began to feel better and experience gratitude and appreciation. I no longer needed the earring to validate that I was loved. So what? I had lost an earring.

That same week, sitting at my desk in my office, I accidentally dropped my pen on the floor. I leaned down to pick up my pen, and there was my earring! When I recounted the story to my family that evening, my father responded with surprise at my being upset. "This earring means nothing. It's just an earring. It doesn't reflect how much I love you. I would have gotten you another one had I known. But in any case, you should know how much I love you."

I went back to the jeweler. Rather than return the earring, I chose to give myself a "love me gift" and had the salesperson turn the diamond stud into a pendant on a necklace.

Your Love Rx for Healing Attachments and Neediness

AWARENESS EXERCISE

Part 1: Awareness of Attachment

Set a timer for five minutes.

Close your eyes.

Inhale deeply.

Exhale completely.

Do this several times as you create your SHIELD.

Bring to mind something that you are attached to, something you feel you need and cannot be without, such as a person, a thing, or a place.

What is it about this person, thing, or place, that makes you feel whole or complete?

Why do you need it so much?

What would happen to you if it disappeared—if, in fact, it isn't gone already?

How would you feel without it?

Would you feel empty without it?

If so, why?

Allow feelings or emotions to rise up for you.

Notice if you are angry or upset.

Notice the sensations in your body, especially your heart.

Ask yourself, ask your heart, why you need this particular person or thing so badly.

Ask to be shown why you feel you are not enough without this person or thing.

Ask to be shown the source of your neediness or emptiness.

When the timer goes off, open your eyes.

Part 2: The Release

Reset the timer for fifteen minutes.

1. Write down your experience and allow yourself to fully observe and witness your feelings. As you write, make a point of
   releasing your emotions and thoughts. Release them so that
   you can eventually release your attachments.
2. When the timer goes off, stop and say, "I now release you from
   my body," as you place your hands on the paper. Then destroy
   the paper. Attachments are difficult to let go. You may want to
   do this exercise for fifteen to twenty minutes every day for
   three to seven days (similar to the Anger Release Journal). Each
   time, follow this exercise with Part 3: Child of Perfection.

Part 3: The Healing: Child of Perfection

You can use the same Child of Perfection healing here as on pages
128–129, making sure you repeat the positive verbal command "I am
enough. I have enough." At the end, before you open your eyes, spend
some time in gratitude, appreciating how much you have in your life
and all that you are.

Daily Reprogramming Tools for Attachment

WHAT TO DO

- Create a SHIELD, visualizing the divine mother telling you
  that you are perfect as you are. Visualize yourself as a child
  being told the same.
- Repeat the Heart Prayer and the Trust Prayer.
- Repeat the positive verbal command "I am enough. I have
  enough."
- Listen to yourself and your needs. Observe as if you are a
  silent witness.
- Do something nice for yourself. This includes giving yourself
  big or small "love me" gifts, such as flowers or your favorite
  cookie.
- Pat yourself on the back often.
- Practice looking in the mirror and saying "You are fabulous!"
  Your body is the only one you have. Appreciate it! Eventually,
  say to yourself as you look in the mirror: "I love you!"

WHEN TO USE THE REPROGRAMMING TOOLS

- When you feel anxious about whether or not something will happen—whether someone will call, if you will get a job, pass an exam, and so on.
- When you feel greedy.
- When you are jealous.
- When you are obsessed with something expensive or nice.
- When you are attached to the way you look.
- When you seek approval.
- When you feel lost or rootless without your external identity—as a lawyer, doctor, mother, etc.
- When you get upset because you have lost something.
- When you are overly concerned with how other people see you.

Goal 3: Overcome addictions, shame, and low self-worth.

ATTACHMENTS TO ADDICTIONS

Everyone has memories or deep wounds stemming from the experience of loss, especially related to the loss or lack of unconditional love in childhood. With these deep wounds, it is difficult to see yourself as whole. You will look for something to fill you up, to make you feel better, to soothe your wounds. You will feel needy or attached. You will find it difficult to let go of people, material possessions, or expectations. You may even develop addictions.

Cravings or addictions, whether food, drugs, sex, or video games, involve a common pathway—the brain reward centers. The brain reward centers hold the memory of how experiences have felt to you, good or bad. When you are feeling bad, the reward center can initiate the behaviors that will help you feel good again.

This sounds reasonable, but here is the catch: when you are desperate, the brain reward centers will do anything to help you feel better.

If you received an abundance of love and affection throughout your life, your brain reward center and other brain areas are likely to predict that your future will be filled with love and abundance. Consequently, you will experience few worries and no cravings, even when you feel bad, because your brain reward center has registered that you possess plenty of reserves from which to pull if necessary.

If, however, you sometimes received love and affection and it was sometimes withdrawn, your brain reward centers experience instability. It registers the message "Now I have, now I don't, now I have, now I don't," creating insecurity. If your reward centers do not trust that you will feel good in the future, they will motivate you toward behaviors that give instant and immediate gratification.

Why?

When the brain reward centers are activated, your dopamine levels rise. When you lose or do not receive the reward you need, your dopamine levels drop. You experience the negative physiology of withdrawal, and your Fear Response is triggered. This motivates you toward reward seeking or addictive behaviors.

Feeling low self-worth is essentially equivalent to having low levels of hormones and neurotransmitters such as oxytocin and dopamine. Your brain reward system is hungry for some relief, to be filled up in any way it can, with food, drugs, sex, exercise, or thoughts. The goal is to return your body to positive physiology, which will eliminate the need for instant gratification that is at the center of all addictions.

 MELINDA: *Breaking Up and Still Addicted*

Melinda was turning thirty when she first came to see me because of worsening depression and anxiety. She was anxious because her therapist of two or three years was going on maternity leave. She also worried that her boyfriend would leave her because they fought incessantly. She complained that her mind raced constantly, she was unable to sleep, and her stomach was a "mess." She also felt she was verging on being an alcoholic because she drank every night to calm her nerves.

On further questioning, Melinda told me that her boyfriend was an alcoholic. He was unreliable and rarely emotionally available, even if he was present physically. He rarely treated her kindly, never paid for anything, and was usually resentful and angry. Melinda took care of him, but the reverse never seemed to occur.

Talking about the imbalance in the relationship brought Melinda to tears. "Why am I obsessing about what he is doing or who he is with? Why am I with him? Why don't I leave him? Why do I care if he leaves me? Why am I so scared to be alone? Why do I feel so horrible and ashamed? Why do I crave alcohol and comfort foods?"

I asked her about her childhood. I discovered that Melinda's anxiety had begun when she was a child, when her parents had had frequent raging fights. Her mother, a "lady of society," was busy drinking martinis at social obligations and rarely around. Her father, although more loving, was home only in the late evenings and frequently away on business. The eldest of three, she and her siblings were left in the care of the housekeeper, and often it was Melinda who looked after her brother and sister.

In her childhood, Melinda essentially learned to feel abandoned and unsupported, initiating feelings of mistrust along with Fear Response activity. In her present life, this translated to low self-worth, neediness, attachment, and fear of abandonment, prompting self-destructive behaviors and addictions.

At this point, I explained to Melinda the concept of Love Reserves. I explained that her reserves were depleted or low because of her childhood history and recent life stresses. I explained that she feared losing her boyfriend because she fantasized that he "completed" her. This fantasy was born out of the insufficient unconditional love from her parents in her childhood. Her lack of love and support from her mother had created a feeling of emptiness that Melinda would forever try to fulfill through a man, alcohol, food, or a fantasy. I explained that until she filled this emptiness with love and self-worth, until she felt whole, her self-destructive patterns would continue.

I taught Melinda the Child of Perfection healing. We especially concentrated on reenacting imagery of the divine mother and father embracing her and offering their unconditional love. I had Melinda go home and practice loving and nurturing the little girl living in her unconscious mind. I asked her to practice the SHIELD, the Trust Prayer, and the Heart Prayer, and, when in need, to use her Love Radar. To help her feel whole, I asked her to contemplate the notion that the love within her was infinite.

Within two weeks of her first visit, Melinda broke up with her boyfriend. She joined Alcoholics Anonymous and began to create a healthy love circle with her friends. Over the next few months, her Love Reserves started to grow and she noted that she felt better, both physically and emotionally. Her only ongoing complaint was that her mind continued to race. She found herself obsessing over what people thought or how situations would turn out, such as a date with a new man. The minute she had a date or went on one, she found herself analyzing and overthinking every move and nuance, wondering if he could be "the one."

I explained to Melinda that when she got this way it was because her mind was low on dopamine. I told Melinda that when she felt needy, fearful, or obsessive and could not stop her mind chatter, she could "think dopamine." She could say to herself, "I am filling up with dopamine." Doing so would at least stop her racing thoughts and possibly stimulate dopamine release. It also could help her detach from her thoughts and reinstitute positive physiology so she could get back to being herself. Indeed, she told me, on her next visit, that just "thinking dopamine" worked!

Melinda stopped expecting every man she met to be "the one" who would "complete" her. She no longer needed someone to complete her. She was whole and complete on her own.

Your Love Rx for Overcoming Loss and Healing Addiction

AWARENESS EXERCISE

Part 1: Awareness of Loss

Set a timer for ten minutes.
Close your eyes.
Inhale deeply.
Exhale completely.
Let go of your thoughts and worries.
Create your SHIELD.
Think about someone or something precious to you that you
    have lost.
Know that you are safe.
It is okay to cry and feel your emotions.
Notice the sensations in your body.
Notice what you feel as you think about what you have lost.
The object of your loss could be a person, a place, or a
    material possession.
It could be a nostalgic feeling.
It could be the loss of your childhood, your innocence,
    your life when it was better, or your health when it was
    better.

It could be the mourning involved in the loss of a feeling of joy or happiness.

Whatever comes up for you, allow yourself to be sad, and allow yourself to grieve.

What is it that you are really missing?

What is it that you are feeling in your heart?

When the timer goes off, stop and open your eyes.

Part 2: The Release

Reset the timer for fifteen minutes.

1. Now write. Let the words pour out of your heart without holding back. Write until you cannot write any more about what you feel you have lost or what is missing for you. Keep writing and see where the words take you. This is your Grief Release Journal.

2. When the timer goes off, place your hands on the words and say, "I now release you from my body." Then destroy the paper. You can continue this exercise for the next few days or as long as you need to, to continue releasing your grief. This may take longer than some of the other exercises. There is no "right" time frame for this healing process.

When you are done, do the following healing.

Part 3: The Healing: Child of Perfection to Infinity: Heal the wounds that are the sources of your addiction

Close your eyes.

Inhale deeply.

Exhale completely.

Create your SHIELD.

The divine mother is standing in this SHIELD.

Her arms of light wrap around you.

Your head rests on her heart as she rocks and cradles you.

You relax and melt into her arms, into her love.

Say the words: "I trust that I am loved and supported and that I am worthy of receiving love," as you allow her to rock, cradle, nurture, and hold you.

Saying those words stimulates the divine mother's heart to send you unconditional love and divine light.

The love and light flow out of her heart into the back of your body, into your chest, and into the right side of your heart.

The love and light fill the entire right side of your chest (including your back).

The love and light spill over into the left side of your heart.

Eventually the left side of your heart is also completely full of love and light, so that the love and light begin to spill back into the right side of your heart.

The light begins to move back and forth from right to left, left to right, in the form of the sign of infinity.

Back and forth, back and forth, creating the sign of infinity.

Repeat the words "I am enough. I have enough. I am whole" over and over again.

Keep repeating these words: "I am enough. I have enough. I am whole."

Your heart is full.

You are whole.

Relax into the fullness of your heart and the fullness of your being for as long as you wish.

Daily Reprogramming Tools for Loss

WHAT TO DO

- Do your SHIELD and repeat the Heart Prayer or Trust Prayer, or repeat any one of the positive verbal commands you have learned so far, such as:
  "I trust that I am loved and supported."
  "I am worthy of receiving love."
  "I am perfect just as I am."
- Reenact the feel of a mother's touch: Create an experience of being held and loved, such as the imagery of a divine mother holding you, so that your mind and body can fully experience receiving unconditional love. Later, you can use this memory to reflect on.
- Create the sign of infinity in your heart.

- Consider grief counseling or a support group as you build a network of support and love around you.
- Make sure that you continue self-care behaviors, such as treating yourself with kindness, eating healthful foods, getting eight hours of sleep, avoiding negative environments and negative people, and exercising regularly.
- Give yourself "love me" gifts.
- Continue writing in your Appreciation Journal.
- Add to your "want list" as you gain clarity of what your needs are.
- Think "dopamine." Repeat to yourself, "Dopamine. I am filling up with dopamine." This is a basic verbal command focused only on your awareness that you are running on empty.

WHEN TO USE THE REPROGRAMMING TOOLS
- When you are upset that you have lost something or someone.
- When you feel lost yourself.
- When you feel nostalgic and it is making you sad or depressed.
- When you have to say good-bye and it upsets you.
- When you are grieving over the end of a relationship.
- When you are grieving over the death of someone you love.
- When you feel abandoned, left behind, or kept out of the picture.
- When you feel lonely.
- When you find yourself seeking comfort or immediate reward by eating a whole cake, calling your ex-boyfriend or -girlfriend, smoking a cigarette, or having a drink.

When you fill up your Love Reserves, you find yourself feeling more confident and secure. You carry yourself more proudly, you speak more assertively, and you respond appropriately, even when you are criticized. You begin to find that you are actually reaching your full potential.

10

SELF-LOVE IN ACTION

Reaching Your Full Potential

W hen you have reached your full potential, you no longer care about what you accumulate or how much others approve or admire you. You accept yourself as complete and perfect as you are, even with your imperfections, and nothing stops you from fully expressing your inner magnificence.

Of course, realizing your full potential requires work. Your next mission is to complete these goals:

1. Learn self-acceptance and self-approval.
2. Overcome approval-seeking behavior and fully express yourself.

Without self-acceptance, you will always seek approval from others. Your dependency on other people's endorsement will cause you to feel angry and hurt when you do not receive it and inhibit you from fully expressing yourself.

This is what I learned about my own lack of self-acceptance.

SEEKING DAD'S APPROVAL

All my life, I have held my father in high esteem. He overcame the hardships inflicted upon him through his life, including escaping persecution for being Jewish in Libya in the late 1940s and early 1950s, then making it to Israel, where he and his family of ten lived in a two-room house whose roof was literally falling in. Despite this challenging start in life, he became not only a successful, world-renowned professor but an amazing cook, mentor, and all-around goofball. Like most parents, he also was always "right."

You can imagine my household when I was a know-it-all teenager! Every time my father told me what to do or think or how to behave, an argument followed. I would react by yelling, pouting, stomping off to my room, and slamming the door, shutting him out and hurting him more than I understood back then.

Over the years, as I learned to love and appreciate myself, I was also able to more fully love and appreciate my father and his life. I was better able to understand that he wanted the best for me and that usually he was trying to protect me from getting hurt. I found that I reacted less and less negatively to his words.

I remember when I excitedly told my father that I had been asked to speak at an important medical conference. My father did not immediately share my excitement and instead offered advice on what I needed to do to be involved in more research opportunities. As he spoke, I noted a little pang of sadness and a small ache in my heart. I remember thinking to myself, "But I am a clinician, not a full research scientist like he is. Why can't I just be who I am?" Though my father was offering me very good advice, his were not the words I wanted to hear at that particular time. I did not want to hear what I should or could be doing. I wanted to hear how wonderful I was, a need that was coming from my own wound, not my father. So while listening to my father's good advice, I imagined that I was embracing my little-girl image, telling her that she was fabulous and magnificent, that I was proud of her and her accomplishments. Immediately, that pang of sadness disappeared, as did the ache. I thanked my father for his advice and for caring. In turn, he replied, "I am so excited for you! I am so proud of you!" And we celebrated! In this way, I was easily able to avoid a battle in a way that I could pass on to patients like Steve.

 STEVE: *Seeking Acceptance*

Steve, then seventeen years old, came to see me feeling very depressed and complaining of headaches and poor sleep. He was already on Prozac since he had been suicidal two years before.

An "A" student in high school in the past, Steve was now barely getting by. He felt he did not belong among his peers, that he was not part of the "group," and like an observer or outsider.

Steve also spoke about having a poor relationship with his father. He was "strict and mean" and, according to Steve, did not approve of Steve or his interests. "I am never good enough for him," he added. He described his mother, in contrast, as loving, affectionate, and supportive.

My heart broke for Steve, and I guided him to become aware of his heart. I asked him what he felt.

Steve described experiencing a constricted feeling in the middle of his chest. He also felt sad and ashamed.

"Why?" I asked. "Why do you feel ashamed? Ashamed of what?"

Steve answered, still with his eyes closed, "I am bad. I am never going to be any good. I am not good enough. My father hates me."

Here was the link! His father had broken his heart and it had closed, probably as a protective measure. The problem was that when his heart closed, he became disconnected from himself and others, which led him to feel like an outsider, even among friends.

I taught Steve how to take care of his little-child self and how to improve his self-care behaviors, such as getting more sleep, exercising, and eating more healthfully. Steve was to practice the SHIELD, the Falling into Self-Love healing visualization (which you will learn below), and the positive verbal command "I love myself. I am enough. I have enough."

On the next visit, three weeks later, Steve was smiling, more animated, and less withdrawn. He reported that he had not felt this good in two years. He was practicing his healing visualization regularly, repeating the positive verbal commands, and journaling. He also watched what he ate and went to the gym. He wanted to decrease the dosage of Prozac he was taking, and he wanted to work on his self-esteem. I was amazed! If only all my patients followed their health plan so well and developed so quickly such insight into what they needed!

Steve, his mother, and I discussed a plan to taper off the Prozac over an extended period, so that he would be completely off the medication by summer. I explained that it would be important for him to stay on his health plan during this process to ensure that he did not have a relapse of depression. I then taught Steve the Trust Prayer and the Child of Perfection healing visualization. I instructed him to practice this visualization in the evening and the Falling into Self-Love visualization in the morning. He was also to repeat the same positive verbal command: "I love myself. I am enough. I have enough."

Initially, Steve's psychiatrist was justifiably against tapering off the Prozac, since Steve had been suicidal in the recent past. Steve, however, began to experience side effects of worsening headaches and tics and small muscle spasms. I suspected that as Steve was getting better, his body was telling us that he did not need such a high dose. Over the course of the next five months, Steve went off Prozac.

He came to see me every month, rain or shine, even when he was sick with a severe case of mononucleosis and a throat infection and probably should have stayed home. I asked him, "What are you doing here? You should be home resting." He replied with a shrug, "I thought maybe you could do some healing work." I smiled, because to me this showed that Steve's heart was healing. He was eager to connect and to receive support and love. I was happy to help.

Steve continued to work on receiving love and learning to love himself and who he was. He also continued to practice the healing visualizations that he learned, the verbal commands, and the self-care behaviors. About two months after his "sick" visit, he walked into my office, looking as if something was on his mind.

The conversation went like this:

ME: What is it you want to tell me?
STEVE (IN AMAZEMENT): How did you know?
ME (SMILING): Now, Steve, it is what people do when they come here. They get things off their minds.
STEVE: I'm gay.
ME: Well, it's about time!
STEVE (SURPRISED): You knew?
ME (SMILING): I guessed. I was waiting for you to believe in yourself, love yourself, and accept yourself enough to admit it to yourself and to the world. Have you told anyone else?

At that point, Steve had only told one other friend. I told him that he needed to remember how loved and supported he was and that it was really safe to tell people like his mother and his brother. Steve did tell his mother, brother, and friends, although he did not tell his father. He knew that it would not go over well, mostly because of his father's fears, not because he, Steve, was a bad person. His father did end up finding out, but not from Steve, so the two never spoke about it. Today, Steve's father still does accept him and his choices.

Fortunately, Steve worked through his father's inability to love him and accept him unconditionally. With more Love Reserves in tow, Steve went off to college happy and openly gay. His mother later told me that someone had written the word GAY on Steve's door. Steve was not concerned. He calmed his mother by letting her know that his roommate had offered to protect him. Steve had found a true friend. He had found himself, and he liked what he found.

Goal 1: Learn self-acceptance and self-approval.

Your Love Rx for Learning Self-Acceptance

AWARENESS EXERCISE

Part 1: Awareness of Lack of Self-Acceptance

You have already done this exercise in various ways throughout this book. By now, many of you have figured out what memory or person is at the source of your shame, blame, or broken heart.

Set a timer for ten minutes.
Sit quietly and ask yourself:

- In what way do I seek approval?
- Do I feel good enough the way I am, or do I need other people or my material acquisitions to confirm to me who I am?
- Do I try to hide anything about myself from others?
- Do I have visions of grandeur—being famous, rich, etc.— to show others how great I am?
- Do I brag about myself and my accomplishments?
- Do I seek compliments?
- Do I look in the mirror and like what I see?
- Why do I need compliments or to be acknowledged?

When the timer goes off, stop.

Part 2: The Release

Reset the timer for fifteen minutes.

1. Write about your answers, your feelings, and what you are beginning to understand. The writing will help you gain clarity. The answers to your questions may not come to you right away, but they may reveal themselves as you write or even later throughout your week. You can write down thoughts or memories in your Awareness Journal or do this exercise several times over the course of the week. As you delve deeper into the answers, you may find that you touch upon something painful, such as feelings of shame or hurt.

2. Stop when the timer goes off and place your hands on the words, saying, "I now release you from my body." This time, you may or may not wish to destroy the paper. You may want to hold on to whatever you write in order to examine it later, to discern how you do not want to be anymore.

Follow this writing exercise with Part 3: Falling into Self-Love.

Part 3: The Healing: Falling into Self-Love

Close your eyes.
Inhale deeply.
Exhale completely.
Create your SHIELD.
Observe your breath. Thank your breath for giving you life today.
Observe your nose. Thank your nose for giving you life today.
Observe your lips. Thank your lips for giving you life today.
Observe your body—all your muscles, skin, bones, internal organs, blood vessels, nerves, brain, cells, and all your imperfections. Thank your body for giving you life today.
Observe your heart. Especially thank your heart for giving you life today.
Observe how you feel.
Acknowledge the feelings and thank them for being there.
The divine light from your SHIELD fills your heart as you breathe in and expands to the rest of your body as you breathe out.
Repeat the words "I love myself. I am enough. I have enough," over and over again.

As you inhale the light and love into your heart and then exhale, the love and light spread throughout the rest of your body.

Do this for as long as you wish.

Daily Reprogramming Tools for Self-Acceptance

WHAT TO DO

- Create your SHIELD regularly, practice the Falling into Self-Love healing.
- Do your Heart Prayer and Trust Prayer exercises.
- Repeat the positive verbal command "I love myself. I am enough. I have enough."
- Improve your self-care behaviors, such as:

  — **Sleep:** Try to set a time for sleep that you stick to every day. Try doing the SHIELD and relaxation techniques prior to going to sleep to clear your thoughts and to feel safe.

  — **Nutrition:** Be good to yourself by eating foods that help you be stronger (such as the Mediterranean diet) and consider adding supplements such as omega-3 fish oils, which prevent inflammation and improve mood and heart health. You may want to meet with a nutritionist and confer with your health care provider about which other supplements would be right for you.

  — **Exercise:** Do some type of aerobic exercise, such as jogging, cycling, basketball, or dancing, and add weight training. Engage in gentle activities to soothe and stretch the muscles. Exercise helps release the neurotransmitters that help elevate your mood. Going outdoors will help you connect to nature and help you connect with your environment. Do something you enjoy. If exercise makes you feel worse (causes body pain or fatigue), start with gentle stretching and walking, even for a few minutes. Yoga and tai chi are wonderful too, especially since you elicit the relaxation response when you do them.

- To help you with self-care, ask yourself before you eat processed food or consume a drink of alcohol: "If I loved myself, would I _____?" For instance, "If I loved myself, would I eat another piece of chocolate cake?"

- Keep your Awareness Journal.
- Keep your Appreciation Journal, focusing on what you appreciate about yourself.
- If you are depressed and having suicidal thoughts or difficulty doing these exercises, please follow up with your doctor or therapist and consider taking an antidepressant if necessary.
- Keep your "want list."

WHEN TO USE THE REPROGRAMMING TOOLS

- When you are seeking approval.
- When you do not feel good enough the way you are, or you need other people or your material acquisitions to confirm to you who you are.
- When you try to hide anything about yourself from others.
- When you have visions of grandeur—being famous, rich, etc.—to show others how great you are.
- When you brag about yourself and your accomplishments.
- When you seek compliments.
- When someone criticizes you.
- When you feel you don't belong.
- When you want to be like everyone else and feel bad that you are not.
- When you are depressed.
- When you feel alone.

THE QUEST FOR ACCEPTANCE AND APPROVAL

Like Steve, most of you still want approval, especially from your parents. Even a small criticism hurts when you are in need of validation. How many times have you announced some sort of exciting idea or news, only to be "shoulded on"—you "should" do this or you "should" do that? How did this make you feel? I know it makes me feel annoyed, defensive, and angry that I am not being listened to or anxious or worried that I have done something wrong. In response, I either say the wrong thing or say nothing at all. I've found, though, a more healthy response to this kind of situation. It seems obvious, but the answer is to learn to express yourself without shame or anger or any other fear-induced defensiveness.

EXPRESSING YOURSELF

When your Fear Response is activated, most of you, like me, will react by saying the "wrong" thing or nothing at all. How many times have you had conversations in your mind of what you should have said or could have said after you had already opened your mouth and offended somebody? Or imagine what you will say to a particular person but never quite manage to say it? How many times have you feared to speak your mind, either because you thought you would be "shoulded on," or you feared that the other person might become angry, you might look or feel stupid, or you might not get the answer you were seeking? You end up telling everyone else but the person who needs to hear your words, thereby creating a larger wave of negativity than if you had just been able to express yourself directly in the first place.

Your ability to speak is your gateway to communicating with the outside world. It is influenced by how others treat you, especially at an early age, when you are developing a sense of self and learning how to communicate your needs. For instance, a child who grows up in a household full of many children may learn that he or she needs to scream or be very creative to be noticed or heard. In the case of a parent or parents who are controlling or abusive in some way (physically, psychologically, or emotionally) and who do not hear or sense the child's needs, the child may shut down his or her voice, fearing to make a sound for fear of reprimand. In either case, the child feels unseen and unheard, not worthy. He either screams out in order to be noticed or shuts down in order to become invisible. Moreover, the culture we live in, in which people who do not fit a certain mold are often judged adversely or ridiculed, may exacerbate this process, so that you may feel too fearful to express yourself freely and truthfully or too angry not to.

Imagine a group of young children running around the home screaming and laughing, totally carefree. Then suddenly a grown-up yells at them to quiet down and frightens them to a halt. Do you remember as a child being hushed or told to behave? Each time you felt judged or afraid to act freely, your voice closed down a bit more. Over time, you learned to close down your desire to express yourself, until you no longer even knew what it was you wanted to express. You learned you were not important enough to have a voice.

Everyone wants to feel special and important. Whether you are an accomplished professional, famous, in a relationship, or alone, you want to feel loved and valued. When you don't feel this way, you cannot fully speak your truth or express yourself or your needs.

When you feel valued, you stand up for yourself. You speak your mind without being on the offensive or defensive. You are not in your Fear Response, so you can have clarity as to what is right for you.

Clarity and self-expression translate into getting what you want. You get the love you want, the support you want, the job you want, and so on. By accepting and approving of yourself, you can express your needs so that somehow the universe seems to work with you to make what you want happen.

Imagine This: Dancing with the Universe

Imagine you are dancing with the universe and you are both trying to lead. You are both trying to express yourselves, worried your point will not get across.

What ends up happening? Do you create resistance or flow? Do you step on each other's toes or do you truly dance?

I like to think that we are dancing the *paso doble* with the universe. In the *paso doble,* the male represents the matador and the female represents the beautiful cape that he gracefully swings around to attract the bull. There is no dance without the matador and not much of a show without the cape. The two have to coexist and move together to achieve the final result; otherwise the matador looks rather silly waving his arms around. You are the beautiful cape. Without you, the dance has no expression. Without you, the universe is not quite the same. You simply need to know this truth to be able to fully and lovingly express yourself.

The Bridge to Self-Expression

Like a detective, you want to search for clues that will lead you to the original wound that led you to believe you were not valuable enough to have a voice. You can start by paying attention to what you long for. Longings are deep-seated desires that have yet to be met. No matter how you try, achieving these longings is a struggle.

Finding the source will allow you to let go of the longings. You may find that perhaps you want something entirely different, something that is easy to acquire. When this happens, it is as if you have found a way to dance with the universe rather than against it and can feel yourself in flow.

 MELODY: *Finding Herself and Her Voice and Getting What She Wanted*

Melody, a forty-four-year-old woman, complained of fatigue, which had recently worsened. "My energy just isn't right," she said. "I have a bone-weary tiredness, and everything hurts." She had been recently diagnosed with diabetes. She had difficulty sleeping and complained of neck and shoulder tension.

Melody had four grown children and had recently divorced. After working as a nurse for many years, she had gone to school full-time. She did miss her home but did not miss the chaos or the turmoil from a disintegrating marriage or the overwhelming responsibility of running the household and keeping the peace. She was eager for the divorce proceedings to be over and wanted nothing from her husband. She just wanted out.

Melody was the oldest of four children. Her parents had fought constantly when home but were otherwise usually absent, both physically and emotionally. Melody, the oldest child, felt she had to look after the other children. She learned to be self-sufficient and responsible from a very young age. She recalled feeling that her needs were not important because they were minor in comparison to other people's needs.

I asked Melody why she did not want anything for herself from the divorce settlement. Why did she want to give everything away? Didn't she have needs? Was this what she really wanted? Did she really deserve nothing and her estranged husband everything? Was she ignoring her needs and giving her power away, as she had in her childhood? I asked her to really think about what she wanted and deserved and to create a "want list," to examine what she longed for and where the longing was coming from. With tears in her eyes, Melody answered, "I long for peace. For love and respect." "So why don't you start by giving it to yourself?" I asked. "Why hurt yourself with the foods you eat, the work regimen you force yourself to maintain, and deny yourself the things you may need from the divorce settlement?" I added, "No one can take away your self-worth. You can only give it away and destroy it yourself."

Melody needed help developing her self-acceptance and self-worth. I taught Melody how to give her little-girl self unconditional love and to heal her heart so she could learn to receive love. I walked her through the Falling into Self-Love healing visualization, the Heart Prayer, the Trust Prayer, and the Child of Perfection healing exercise over the course of two visits. She was to create her SHIELD and use the positive verbal command "I love myself. I am enough. I have enough. I am perfect as I am."

Melody was also to start a manifestation collage so that she could begin to create the destiny her heart desired.

THE MANIFESTATION COLLAGE

A Manifestation Collage is your chance to express yourself and be creative. It involves taking your "want list" and your self-portrait and creating the world you want to see yourself in and the person you see yourself as. Use magazine clippings, photographs, anything visual. You can envision a sexy image of yourself, a stoic picture, a sweet picture. Do as many as you like. At any given moment, any one of you is kind, mean, strong, vulnerable, smart, clueless, and on and on. None of these things defines you. You can be a painter, a skier, a banker—all of the above. Use your imagination, and mix it in with your own real world.

Over the next two months, Melody told me that she continued to practice her SHIELD, the visualizations, and the positive verbal commands. She was exercising and following a better diet. She felt increasingly sure of herself and what she wanted. Melody made a list of what she wanted from her husband. Her fatigue had improved, but she still had tension in her neck.

I asked Melody if she was nervous or stressed about anything. More specifically, I wanted to know if she was angry about anything that she was not able to express. Melody nodded, commenting that she was anxious about the upcoming meeting with her husband, the two lawyers, and the judge the following week. This meeting would finalize the divorce settlement and decide who would get what. She worried whether her demands would be met, but she was mostly upset with her ex-husband for even challenging the demands.

"What do you long for out of this court hearing, Melody?" I asked.

She answered, "I want to be justly heard and get what I am asking for."

"What are you scared of?" I asked further.

"I am scared of being invisible again—like when I was a child," she replied.

I guided Melody to fill her heart with divine love and support and with compassion, then radiate that love to her little-girl image, following the Perfect As I Am healing visualization (which you will learn shortly).

One week later, she was pain-free. She also happily reported that her divorce was finally settled. The judge had awarded her everything she requested and more. When the judge had in fact called her husband "cheap," Melody truly did feel supported, loved, and seen. She felt an enormous sense of freedom, as if she had been cut free of the bindings and longings that had prohibited her from expressing herself.

Goal 2: Overcome approval-seeking behavior and fully express yourself.

Your Love Rx for Expressing Yourself

AWARENESS EXERCISE

Part 1: Awareness of Longing

Write down a list of the things you long for, what you most deeply desire. Then choose the one most significant longing—the one that causes you to feel sad, upset, and anxious when you think about how much you want it.

Set a timer for five minutes.
Close your eyes.
Inhale deeply.
Exhale completely.
Create your SHIELD.

Focus on your heart.

Think about your longing.

What do you feel in your chest?

What does longing feel like?

Is it a pull? An ache? A tense feeling?

Find the spot in your chest, or your heart, where you feel the
longing feeling.

Once you find the spot, imagine a rope tied to it.

The rope is extremely long.

Pick up the rope and begin to follow its length.

It is extremely long.

When you get to the other end, see yourself as an infant, a
child, or a young adult.

You are at the source of your longing.

You are at the source of not having enough or being enough.

What do you see? What do you feel? What are the
circumstances?

When the timer goes off, stop.

Part 2: The Release

Reset the timer for fifteen minutes. You may or may not want to work
with a partner, as ultimately, this exercise is to help you with self-
expression. If you do not work with a partner, you can sit in front of
a mirror. If you cannot listen to yourself, who can?

1. Sit face-to-face with your partner if you have one or look in the
   mirror. Place your right hand on your own heart and your left
   hand on your partner's (or your reflection's) heart. Say these
   words to each other: "I hear you."
2. Each person takes turns telling the other what he or she discovered and felt, while the other person listens without inter-
   rupting or thinking about his or her own story. You will have
   your turn. Simply listen.
3. If you are doing this exercise alone, listen to yourself lovingly.
   Do not judge or repress. Listen as if you were listening to the
   most important person in your life. When you are each done,
   thank each other for listening and say, "I have now released my
   longing from my body."

You may both wish to spend some time writing about your feelings and your experiences in your Awareness Journal.

Part 3: The Healing: Perfect as I Am

> Close your eyes.
> Inhale deeply.
> Exhale completely.
> Create your SHIELD.
> The divine light from the SHIELD fills your heart with love and compassion as you inhale.
> The light and love expand throughout your entire body as you exhale.
> Repeat these words silently to yourself several times: "I love myself, I am enough. I have enough."
> Bring up your imagery of your little child.
> Embrace him or her, speak to him or her lovingly, and surround him or her with the SHIELD as you say to the child, "I see you. I hear you. You are perfect as you are."
> The divine light and love from the SHIELD fill your little child's heart as he or she inhales and expands through his or her little body as he or she exhales.
> Continue to say to the child, "I see you. I hear you. You are perfect as you are."
> As you both fill with love and light, your images merge into one image.
> Repeat these words several times: "I am perfect as I am."
> Do this as long as you wish.

Daily Reprogramming Tools for Releasing Longings

WHAT TO DO
- Create your SHIELD.
- Practice the Falling into Self-Love healing visualization, then add the little-child imagery to complete the Perfect as I Am healing visualization.
- Repeat the positive verbal command "I love myself. I am enough. I have enough" and add, "I am perfect as I am."

- Use any of the prayers that feels right for you.
- Continue writing in your Appreciation Journal.
- Add to your want list and create a Manifestation Collage that you can add to every day.

WHEN TO USE THE REPROGRAMMING TOOLS
- When you feel a longing in your heart for something that seems impossible to get.
- When you feel your needs are not being met.
- When you feel frustrated with your life, and unsatisfied with what you have or who you are.
- When you are jealous of what others have.
- If you are constantly comparing yourself to others.
- When you feel you are not being treated fairly.
- When you feel you are not getting your point across or no one is listening to you.
- When you feel as though you were invisible.

ENHANCE YOUR SELF-EXPRESSION THROUGH CREATIVITY

Your prescription, as you begin to feel more accepting and loving toward yourself, is to remember what it was like to be a child. My niece, Maia, being five years old, is not self-conscious yet and often dances around without a care, screams at the top of her lungs, or walks around wearing a striped rainbow-colored shirt, a taffeta fuchsia skirt with "bling" or rhinestones, silvery shoes with bows, and red-and-pink tights. She is a fashion queen! Use your imagination.

- Turn on the music really loud and dance!
- Buy some crayons and big sheets of paper and draw—no one is watching and no one is judging.
- Do something spontaneous.
- Giggle in the middle of the grocery store, just because you can.
- Spend a few minutes or more each day pretending to look at the world through the eyes of a five-year-old.
- Look up at the clouds and try to make out their shapes.
- Write the story of you in your journal.

- Take a class in some kind of creative activity. If you don't like it, quit and try something else until you find something you enjoy.

Everyone expresses themselves in different ways. It may be through music, dance, painting, or it may be through public speaking, writing, innovative ideas or thinking, playing chess, etc. Being creative simply involves allowing whatever is on the inside to be expressed on the outside, much like buds that bloom into beautiful flowers. Remember that no two flowers are the same. One is not better or worse than the other. The flowers express themselves differently as they grow. For this reason, a large part of your daily reprogramming will involve expressing yourself creatively.

REACHING YOUR FULL POTENTIAL IS SELF-LOVE

Each and every one of us is different. Each and every one of us has a different genetic makeup, different life experiences, and different filtering systems that help us understand our world. Each and every one of us breathes in the same air, lives in the same universe and on the same earth, and has the ability to receive and give the same love. Each and every one of us is a vessel that takes in the same surrounding energy, but because you are built differently, you express that energy in your own individual way. You are part of a larger whole, and also your own unique person.

By building your Love Reserves and increasing your ability to live in flow, become whole, approve of yourself, and express yourself, you may find that you also manifest the destiny that your heart desires and get what you want.

11

COMPLETING THE LOVE

Spiritual Love

Think about someone you love who is no longer alive—perhaps a grandparent, a favorite relative, or a teacher. Picture this person comforting you as she or he did when you were younger. See the wrinkles their eyes make as they smile at you. Appreciate this person's wonderful qualities. Allow yourself to be comforted. Allow yourself to surrender into this person's arms.

You have just managed to connect with something that extends beyond your everyday reality, what I call Spiritual Love. It is the love that has no boundaries in time and space and allows you to relate to all things and all beings.

Spiritual Love opens you to the wonders of life. As Social Love connects you to others and Self-Love connects you to yourself, Spiritual Love connects you to something larger than yourself, such as nature, God, or Spirit. This experience helps you feel relaxed and secure and less angry, alone, and fearful, as if your mother or father were holding you, keeping you nurtured and safe.

With Spiritual Love, you are better able to find meaning in any situation and the courage to deal with it successfully. You develop a deep sense of yourself. You discover that you are part of a larger whole and without your part in it, this larger whole is incomplete.

You don't have to be religious or believe in God or any other spiritual form to experience Spiritual Love, as my patient Michael discovered.

Michael: *Golf*

Michael was eighty-three years old, a retired businessman and avid golfer. He was vacillating between being an agnostic and an atheist. He initially saw me because his wife was worried about his health. He was not sleeping, his blood pressure was high, and he was anxious and depressed.

When I asked him why he might be anxious or depressed, Michael told me that he constantly worried about his own death. He worried about dying because he felt that he had not left a "name"; he had not contributed anything to the world and was afraid that he would be easily forgotten one day. He did not believe in God, he did not believe his spirit would continue to exist after death, and he was very concerned about what would happen after he died. Therefore, he said, his mind raced at night and he could not sleep.

In our discussion, I asked Michael to tell me about his support network, about his friends and family, and what they meant to him. As he started telling me about them, his face lit up. I commented that it sounded as though he loved and was loved by many people. I asked him to think about all this love that he had in his life and then examine how his chest felt. He admitted that his chest felt good. It felt open and light. I said, "There you go! There is the awesome connection that you can't see or hear but feel right in your heart. This magical feeling that transcends time and space is called love. Love will always live on. You will exist always in the hearts of those who love you, and they in yours."

Michael smiled, liking that answer, but of course, he still had many questions and concerns. He was a practical businessman, and this answer was a bit hokey for him, even though he did admit to feeling those pleasant sensations in his heart. He went on to say that he was still worried. Even though his family and friends loved him, he felt he had not done enough for the world. He believed himself to be selfish.

I asked him if he had ever contributed his time or help, money, or volunteered for any person or community. I believe it took at least twenty minutes (or so it seemed) for him to list the many people and places he had helped or offered service to. I was amazed. I asked him why he thought he had not done enough, when he so clearly had given so much. Michael replied that he could have done better, he could do more. I asked him why he felt this way, and after a little probing, he finally answered that he felt unworthy and somehow not good enough. He also admitted that my pointing out all that he had done and given made him feel better about himself. He had never thought about it this way.

Michael then wanted to know how he could sustain feeling this good. He knew that as soon as he left the office, he would go back to worrying, feeling alone and unworthy. I instructed him to remember to connect to that love that sat in his heart and to remember that it sits in the hearts of others as well.

I encouraged him to frequently engage in activities where friends and family surrounded him, to continue volunteering as he already was, and to start paying attention to how all these activities gave him the feeling that he was connected to something much larger than himself.

Michael found this instruction to be very curious and asked me, "How will I know what that is? How will I know when I am connected to something larger? I don't really get it." I replied that he had likely already experienced it. He looked at me dumbfounded. I reminded him that he was an avid golfer. I asked him to remember his feelings and experiences when he plays golf on a beautiful day with his good friends and he hits the most perfect drive: it is like any other moment that should be captured in time. The angels sing. The sea parts. You do not even notice that you are breathing. It feels as though all is one and you are one with everything around you. Athletes call this "being in the zone." This, I told Michael, is spirituality and what it feels like to be connected to something larger than oneself. The more he made this connection, the more he would appreciate the love that is in and around him, the better he would feel about himself and the happier and healthier he would be.

CONNECTING TO SOMETHING LARGER THAN YOURSELF

Receiving love and support from others and giving it to them translates into reaching out beyond yourself, which helps you understand and believe that you are not alone. The profound sense that you belong to a larger whole is one of the characteristics associated with physical, emotional, and mental resilience. This belief leads you to be more courageous, adaptive, better able to perform effectively even under stress, and more altruistic. Interestingly, this profound sense that you are connected to yourself and to others comprises the definition of spirituality.

Religion is one of the main paths to spirituality. The Latin root *religio* signifies the bond between humanity and a greater-than-human power. The difference between religion and spirituality is that the latter is something more abstract and the former is a definable, structured, and human-made system. Although some people view the system's structure to have faults, many of the spiritual practices embraced by religion confer health benefits. One of them is prayer.[1] Some studies show an inverse relationship between frequently attending religious services and mortality.[2] That is, the more often you go, the longer you live. Other research has found lower rates of high blood pressure in individuals who attend religious services.[3] Religion and spirituality also bestow a sense of community, extending the Social Love aspect of your Love Pyramid.

 ISABELLE: *Missing Mom*

Isabelle came to see me appearing distraught and sad, tears welling up in her eyes. I asked her what was wrong, and she replied that she was thinking about her mother, who had died two years previously. She complained that her "heart felt heavy" and that she was experiencing shortness of breath and lack of sleep.

I knew that I could not possibly understand her loss, especially since I could not and did not want to imagine life without my mother. How lonely it must be without one's mother, to be without the love and nurturing qualities that a mother can give. You never outgrow the need for these virtues. You are never too old to receive them, even when you become a mother yourself.

Rather than concentrate on how bad she felt, I asked Isabelle to spend some time contemplating all the gifts and beauty with which her mother had enriched her life. Since Isabelle also frequently went to church, I asked her to include her mother in her prayers and to pray to continue to receive all the wonderful things that she had experienced with her mother when she was alive. I encouraged Isabelle to reflect on her own values and where they had come from, especially all the things that her mother might have instilled within her, things that were precious and could never be removed or lost. I also encouraged her to join a grief support group.

Isabelle did what I prescribed. She returned a few weeks later, already beginning to feel better. She told me that when she prayed, she experienced her mother's essence, feeling that she connected with a profound sense of love and wholeness. She also joined a support group in her church and found the love and connection with others to be very nurturing and helpful. Over time, Isabelle began to heal her grief. She allowed herself to express that she felt alone without her mother and took measures to help herself feel more whole, despite the loss. She did so by receiving love and support from others and by connecting with the love she gave and received from the God she believed in. As her physiology changed, she was able to feel better and better, physically, psychologically, and emotionally.

How Spiritual Love Helped Me

During my own experiences of depression, I was disconnected from others, from myself, and especially from Spiritual Love. I didn't understand why so many bad things were happening to me and why I was "being punished." I lost faith in my ability to create change and in the universe's willingness to support me. I felt victimized rather than loved and supported. I did not allow myself to hope, dream, or imagine that anything could be different, because when I did get my hopes up, I found myself devastated and disappointed. I was too exhausted to believe anymore.

But as the people around me rallied and supported and cared for me, I grew to understand that I was loved. I then allowed myself to imagine and hope. I began to connect to something larger than myself. I started by connecting with Nature.

Try It

Walk outside or look at a photo of a beautiful landscape of nature, or simply imagine a lovely natural setting when you close your eyes.

Now appreciate all that you see, feel, sense, smell, or taste.

Appreciate how amazing and awesome nature is.

Appreciate that as you look at nature, you can see that its state is one of constant flow: Night follows day. Autumn follows summer. One flower blooms as another wilts and withers, feeding the soil to bring about new growth. Nothing is permanent, and nothing is static.

Appreciate how nature shows no resistance to this impermanence, only flow.

Now appreciate how connected you are to nature. You are part of nature. You are part of this flow.

You have just connected to something larger than you and, inadvertently, also appreciated yourself.

When you lose your will or desire to imagine, to dare to believe that life can be full of love and joy, you disconnect from the notion that you belong to a larger whole. You separate from Spiritual Love. This larger whole does not need to be God or Spirit or the divine. This "larger whole" refers to your imagination and dreams, your belief in the future; that some force larger than you is working with you to manage uncertainty; that you do not stand alone, just as no molecule stands alone.

When you feel that you are not alone, you are more likely to experience yourself as full, whole, and complete. You can then reach out and help others who are in need.

SPIRITUAL AFFECTION: REACHING OUT TO HELP SOMEONE WHO HOLDS NO IMMEDIATE BENEFIT FOR YOU

Altruism, the act of helping someone with whom you have no relationship, who is neither family nor friend, who offers no apparent benefit to you, is what I call "spiritual affection." The way that loving touch is the action that flows from Social Love and self-nurturance is the action that flows from Self-Love, altruism is the action that flows from Spiritual Love. You are the ultimate beneficiary of your altruistic acts. The benefits may not be immediate, tangible, or quid pro quo, but the feelings of self-worth and contribution produced by altruistic acts reverberate throughout your being and stimulate the Love Response.

For instance, volunteering by older adults has a protective effect on mortality.[4] Older adults who give social support to others are more inclined to live longer than older adults who receive support.[5] Not only do volunteers live longer, they also feel better. Known as the "helper's high," the experience of helping others creates a sense of calm and freedom from stress by turning off the Fear Response. Many "helpers" experience a slower heart rate and lower blood pressure[6] and may also benefit by improved immune response.[7]

Indeed, these physiological changes that occur with altruistic works are the basis of the sense of warmth or the experience of "helper's high." Acts of giving increase activity in the brain's reward centers, releasing the "feel-good" chemicals such as dopamine and endorphins.[8] Reaching out and helping someone results in real health benefits, especially in decreasing the effects of fear and the Fear Response.

As His Holiness the Dalai Lama has stated: "If you shift your focus from yourself to others, extend your concern to others, and cultivate the thought of caring for others, then this will have the immediate effect of opening up your life and helping you to reach out." In caring for others, you feel you are making a difference in the world. You experience a stronger sense of control and a better ability to make meaning of your situation. And, perhaps most important, you experience less fear.

IMAGINE THIS SCENARIO

Your flight is leaving in thirty minutes, and you still have to get through the security line, which seems to extend for miles. Your Fear Response has you in overdrive, and you are freaking out!

Suddenly, one of the security staff notices your panic-stricken face and asks if you are okay. You explain your problem, and the staff members immediately whisk you through the line and you board the plane on time.

Feeling more at ease and thankful that someone helped you, you see that a family is upset that they have not been seated together. You offer your seat and move. Not only do you make their day, but now the thankful flight attendant pays extra-special attention to you to ensure your comfort.

Would you have offered your seat had you made it onto the plane still stressed and resentful? How differently would this scenario have played out?

Building the Spiritual Love side of your Love Pyramid has a "tickle effect," whereby one nice act feeds another; one heart tickles another heart, which tickles another, and so on. We are all connected, and it is Spiritual Love that reminds us of that each and every time we practice it.

As with Social Love and Self-Love, strengthening Spiritual Love involves learning some basics that you can then put into action. Your first step is to work on developing a trust in this bigger connection and to establish your ability to believe and imagine.

Spiritual Love contributes to your Love Reserves. With more Love Reserves and a larger cushion of love for yourself, your love will overflow onto others, cushioning them as well. The secret is to perform acts of kindness simply because you can. Your Love Response will run at full throttle, and others will notice the difference in you.

12

SPIRITUAL LOVE BASICS

Learning to Believe

Sometimes, no matter how many people love you and no matter how much you practice self-care, you still feel bad. Self-love talk, self-care exercises, friends, and family are not enough to pull you out of your darkness. Your Fear Response is so persistent and your negative physiology is so prominent that the imbalance within you is difficult to fix.

Have you had times when nothing seemed to make you feel better? Have you automatically reached for a cigarette, a drink, or a piece of chocolate or gone for a run in an attempt to feel better and numb your discomfort?

This is when Spiritual Love comes in.

Spiritual Love enhances your cushion of love. It builds up your Love Reserves. Then you can face the darkness of your suffering without feeling that you are about to fall into a big black abyss and never return. You can use your Love Reserves to support you while you address your fears and anguish and wipe out the darkness.

To create the Spiritual Love part of your Love Pyramid, your mission is to meet these four goals:

1. Develop trust in the unknown and what you do not understand.
2. Learn how to believe in the existence of something larger than yourself and rediscover faith.

3. Face and heal the wounds that are the source of your suffering.
4. Heal by connecting to Heaven and Earth.

Goal 1: Develop trust in the unknown and what you do not understand.

DEVELOPING SPIRITUAL TRUST

Spiritual Love means allowing yourself to connect with all that is divine, good, and protective and letting it hold you and comfort you. Like a baby, you learn to fall into the arms of something larger than you, something divine and loving, to hold you for a while—not to change anything but just to hold you so that your physiology can regulate itself and you can see your situation more clearly.

Remember playing the "trust fall" game as a child? When your friends stood behind you and you had to fall back, trusting that they would catch you?

Just like the "trust fall" game, connecting with Spiritual Love involves letting go. You let go of your expectations that your situation will change or that something will be fixed. Instead, you surrender to something that is beyond you, that connects you to all things, trusting that this something is working for you, not against you.

Think of it as a kind of Spiritual Trust fall. I'll tell you how it worked for me.

REDISCOVERING MY FAITH

A few years ago, I had a profound experience while meditating. That day, I felt exhausted. I had just returned from an emergency trip to Israel to see my father. A month previously, my father had given the family a scare, suffering a heart attack while on business in Paris. I took on the responsibility of contacting his doctors and making sure his medical records got to the right hands in Paris. He ended up having a procedure done while there. He seemed to be doing well, so his doctors approved his travel to Israel. While in Israel, he suffered another small heart attack, and I found myself tearfully flying to Israel, wondering if it would be the last time I saw him. Once again, I found myself coordinating his care and spending hours on the phone in the middle of the night.

My siblings and I flew fourteen hours and spent an intense five days with my father and mother. We were relieved to see that he would recover, and I tried to enjoy my time with him, as much as I could. By the end of the trip I was exhausted—physically, mentally, and emotionally. I also felt an overwhelming depression come over me.

Despite knowing that my father was okay and that I had much support and love from family and friends, I felt miserable. I felt alone, and I wanted to withdraw from everything. I was tired of trying so hard to "make things right." I was tired of trying to fix people and make life better. I couldn't save my father. I couldn't save anyone. Why bother? I started finding faults in myself and in others. Everything and everyone upset or irritated me.

I tried creating my SHIELD, doing my Heart Prayer and Trust Prayer, and I still felt awful. I continued to meditate.

I examined the heaviness in my heart. I asked my heart to show me the wound that was creating my sadness and pain. The vision I had was of me, hanging, about to fall, from the top of a castle wall. I struggled to hang on because if I let go, I would fall to my death. I had to choose to either let go and fall to my peril or pull myself over the wall so that I could stand on the roof of the castle, taking the risk that I might be trespassing and get caught.

After much deliberation, I chose to pull myself over, onto the roof. But when I did pull myself over, I found that I still could not let go of the wall because I was standing in a rapidly moving river. Again, I found that I had two choices—I could either let go, perhaps to my peril, or continue the struggle to hold on by hanging on to the wall.

What was this metaphor? I asked myself. What was this vision trying to tell me? I finally figured out that I had a choice to make: Did I want to live or did I want to die? If I wanted to live, was I going to spend my life doubting that I would be okay, that things happened as they should, and that I had the resources to handle whatever should happen? If I continued to distrust, my entire life would be a struggle, and I would go nowhere.

I knew that either way, whether standing in the river or hanging on the wall, I would have to take a leap of faith at some point and let go. I would have to trust that I did not have all the answers and that not all solutions are always apparent. I would have to let go at some point and trust that the outcome would be the right one for me. My only choice was, did I want to live, or die? If I wanted to live, I would have to learn to trust and not try to control my life or anyone else's.

I let go of the wall in my heart, not because I wanted to die but because I wanted to live. I wanted to trust. I said to myself, "Relax into love," and I let go. I did the Spiritual Trust fall and found myself relaxing in a pool of crystal blue water. I felt no pain, sadness, or depression. I felt that I was floating and at peace.

I wanted to see what might have happened had I let go of the wall in the first instance. I brought back the image of myself hanging to the wall with nothing below me. I did the Spiritual Trust fall and let go as I said to myself, "Relax into love." Rather than falling to my peril, I flew. I began to soar like an eagle, feeling confident that I had the resources to handle whatever hardship I was to face. I understood that I might not be able to change my situation, fix my father, or heal others, but I could trust that the universe would work with me to make sure I had enough love reserves and resources. I felt free.

When I came out of my meditative state, I felt lighter, as if a heavy weight had lifted. I still had my fears and concerns, but now I had faith. I made the decision to live my life in service, in giving and teaching others about love and healing, without trying to change them or anything else.

Within a month, my life began to change drastically. I began writing this book, and many new opportunities came my way. This is not to say that I did not have relapses. I learned, though, that when I did feel depressed, I didn't need to try to fix anything but instead "relax into love" and do the Spiritual Trust fall into my SHIELD, so that those periods of depression went from lasting for months to weeks to days to hours and finally to minutes.

Try It

Inhale deeply.
Exhale completely.
Create your SHIELD.
The divine light surrounds you and holds you.
Unconditional love surrounds and comforts you.

There is nothing you need to do or be.
You are completely safe.
Say to yourself, "Relax into love."
Imagine you are falling backward into the pool of
    divine light.
Let go and fall back.
Relax into love.

Goal 2: *Learn how to believe in the existence of something larger than yourself and rediscover faith.*

LEARNING TO BELIEVE

Your brain's prediction that "all will be well" in your future requires that you have experiences throughout your lifetime where you feel that the universe was working for you rather than conspiring against you, through either "happy coincidences" or periods when you have had strokes of "good luck." When such positive occurrences do not happen and you are let down or disappointed, you are more likely to feel victimized and persecuted, anxious, apprehensive, and helpless. You may feel as if everything in your life has been and will continue to be a struggle, as if you are constantly swimming upstream.

 JUSTINE: *Experiencing Is Believing*

When Justine came to see me, she had difficulty sitting still, shifting around constantly in her seat. She was forty-two years old and in the past year had undergone an operation to remove breast cancer. She complained that she worried constantly, so much so that it had become physically debilitating. She worried about her children, about her work, about her husband, and about their finances, even though there were sufficient funds in their account. To her, danger lurked everywhere. It was wearing her down. She was exhausted, especially since she awoke at least twice a night to check on her children.

When I asked her about her childhood, Justine reported that she was the oldest of three children and had been the center of her parents' universe. They expected only the best from her, and she remembered feeling a lot of pressure to live up to their expectations, striving for perfection. Justine was expected to attend the best schools and aim for a lucrative career, while also getting married and having children. A devout atheist and scientist, her father refused to allow even the traditional Jewish celebrations into the family home. He was also manic-depressive, and during his relapses he became paranoid, trusting no one, even his family. Everything had to be scientifically proven and everyone had to prove themselves, including Justine. She worked hard to meet her father's expectations, worried that if she did not, her father might have one of his manic or depressive episodes.

Justine herself did not believe that there existed a God or a higher power that could share in the responsibility. To her, there was no proof in her life that such an entity existed. Instead, she was driven by her fears of "what if": What if I don't succeed? What if something bad happens? What if I cannot control the outcome and then, when something bad happens, it will be my fault?

I taught Justine to use the SHIELD, Heart Prayer, and Trust Prayer. I chose healing visualizations that would help her connect with her imagination in order to plant the seed of possibility that perhaps something larger did exist beyond what her eyes could see or science could explain. I taught her the Mother Earth visualization and encouraged her to spend time in nature. These activities would help her connect to the notion that she was a part of something much larger than herself. We created a program for self-care that would enable her to rebuild her physical strength.

On her next visit, Justine said she was amazed at how much better she felt. She was getting more sleep, and she felt less tired. She was surprised how aware she was becoming of her attitudes, actions, and behaviors. She reported that when she and her husband and children had driven by Harvard University one day, she had said to her daughter, "Look, honey, you could go here one day." The second the words came out of her mouth, she realized that she was putting the same pressure on her daughter that her father had put on her. She was upset with herself, as she did not want her daughter to think that she had to go to Harvard, as she had. She wanted her to know that she would still love her, whatever path she chose in life. So she immediately added, "If that is what you want, when you are old enough to decide. You can go anywhere you want."

Justine said that incident made her "more determined to make changes now." She really wanted to know how to get her mind to finally stop worrying and turn off the constant negative babble in her head. She wanted to trust more and think less. I offered her the following exercise to help her quiet her mind. Go ahead and try it yourself.

AN EXERCISE FOR ACTIVE BRAIN SYNDROME AND QUIETING THE MIND

Create your SHIELD.

The light is shining upon you.

Imagine that a beam of light is shining onto the crown of your head and into your mind into the middle of your forehead.

Imagine this beautiful light expanding outward from the middle of your forehead, expanding and filling your mind.

It begins to radiate in all directions and begins to open the crown of your head.

It then emerges out of the crown of your head and joins with the light from the sky above.

The effectiveness of this exercise stunned Justine. She said she couldn't remember the last time she had experienced such peace and quiet. I told her she could do this exercise anytime and anyplace. The exercise would also help her establish a connection with something more "ethereal," without having to believe in anything specific.

On her subsequent visits, Justine reported that she was worrying less and that her husband had commented that she was more pleasant to be around. She said that she still had fears, but she was aware of them and felt more capable of working through them. She felt less debilitated. She also added that she was starting to believe that just maybe there was something out there—something that was beyond her ability to comprehend. And whatever this something was, it wasn't so bad.

Your Love Rx for Trusting and Believing

AWARENESS EXERCISE

Part 1: Awareness of Belief

In this exercise, you will examine what you do and do not believe in. Spend some time contemplating each of the following questions. You may be surprised at what you discover. Notice which questions elicit the most profound reactions or emotions.

Ask yourself: Do I or do I not believe . . .

- In a higher power? That something larger than me exists?
- In God, in several gods, a divine presence, Buddha, Jesus, Mohammad, Mother Nature? Does my higher power have a face?
- That everything that happens to me, good and bad, happens for a reason?
- That everything that happens to me is for the good, never the bad?
- That I am ultimately connected to all things?
- That I am ultimately alone and on my own?
- That the universe acts to help me get what I want?
- That the universe doesn't care about me and often works against me?
- That the universe has nothing to do with how I get what I want?
- That the universe loves and supports me?

Part 2: The Release

When you finish contemplating these questions, set a timer for fifteen minutes.

1. Write about your experience—what you have discovered and noticed. Do not judge yourself or repress your thoughts.
2. When the timer goes off, stop, place your hands on the words, and say, "I now release you from my body." Destroy the paper this time. Follow this release with Part 3: Mother Earth.

Part 3: The Healing: Mother Earth

Close your eyes.
Inhale deeply.
Exhale completely.
Create your SHIELD.

Imagine that as you exhale, your body melts into the
   earth.
With every exhale, allow your body to relax and melt into
   the arms of Mother Earth.
Let go. Surrender into her arms with every breath.
Say to yourself, "Relax into love."
You are safe, protected, and loved.
Say these words: "I trust that I am loved and supported."
With every breath, feel your body melting into the ground,
   into the arms of Mother Earth.
Sink deeper and deeper into the earth, into the arms of
   Mother Earth.
Say to yourself, "Relax into love."
Your entire body melts into the earth, into the arms of
   Mother Earth.
Your head, mind, neck, and face melt into the
   earth.
Your chest and back, abdomen and pelvis melt into the
   earth.
Your arms, legs, hands and feet, fingers and toes melt into
   the earth.
Let go, surrendering into her arms.
You feel loved, safe, and supported.
Say these words: "I trust that I am loved and supported."
You receive nurturance and strength from the earth.
Allow yourself to receive nurturance and strength.
Feel it rise from the earth into your body.
You are becoming strong and able.
Say these words: "I trust that I am loved and supported."

Daily Reprogramming Tools for Trusting and Believing

WHAT TO DO
- Create your SHIELD.
- Say the positive verbal commands "I trust that I am loved and
  supported" and "Relax into love."
- Imagine that you are relaxing or melting into the arms of
  Mother Earth.
- Imagine that the crown of your head opens up to receive the di-

vine light that fills your mind and body with light and unconditional love.

- Practice breath exercises.
- Keep your Appreciation Journal, to help you be constantly aware of all that you have and all that you are.
- Practice self-care by getting adequate sleep, following appropriate nutrition and exercise programs, and seeking medical care when necessary.
- Spend time outdoors, connecting with nature.
- Spend time with those you love.

WHEN TO USE THE REPROGRAMMING TOOLS

- When you have "active brain syndrome" or worry too much.
- When you are filled with anxiety.
- When you cannot sleep.
- When you are trying too hard to control something or someone.
- When you feel you have the sole responsibility to make sure everyone is okay or everything turns out all right.
- When you feel alone and helpless.
- When you do not feel supported.
- When you feel you are being criticized and cannot handle it.
- When you have a lot of pain in your muscles and joints because you are always bracing yourself for uncertainty.
- When your immune system keeps breaking down (you get frequent colds, etc.).

BELIEVE WITHOUT BEING BLIND: SPIRITUAL TRUST VERSUS BLIND TRUST

People with negative childhood experiences usually have difficulty trusting. They learn that nothing and no one can be trusted. They fear uncertainty and prefer to try to control their world and everything around them. They either defy all rules or stick by them religiously, not questioning but trusting the authority that created them.

This is blind trust, and it is very different from Spiritual Trust. Spiritual Trust means believing that you possess sufficient resources to handle uncertainty. Spiritual Trust refers to a spiritual quality, being able to surrender to the idea that there exists something larger than yourself, something that will hold and love you, so that you can be certain that everything that happens, happens for good.

Blind trust has just the opposite effect. It is not beneficial for your survival. With blind trust, you do not listen to your own instincts and instead trust a predator's intentions when he or she invites you into their den.

Blind trust occurs when you are in so much fear or pain that you desire someone or some higher being to take care of it for you. Your Love Reserves are so low or nonexistent that you reach out for any help from any quarter. You give the full responsibility and trust not to yourself but to a higher power or authority. In giving up your own power, you may actually feel more victimized and helpless. Then, when God or a higher authority appears to let you down, you feel betrayed and abandoned, triggering old wounds from when this happened to you in your past; triggering the belief that love is given when you are "good" and taken away when you are "bad."

Spiritual Trust comes from knowing you have a large cushion of love that will break your fall and comfort you, should you falter. It comes from appreciating that a lifetime of positive experiences has confirmed to you that you are loved and supported and that you have ample Love Reserves. You are able to do the Spiritual Trust fall and relax into love.

ERIC: *Finding Faith and Relaxing into Love*

Eric, forty-five years old, came to see me complaining that he had tried modifying his diet and exercising, but his blood pressure was still high. He was reluctant to start medications and wanted to find other ways to reduce his blood pressure. He complained of chronic lower back pain and a history of herniated discs and difficulty falling asleep as his mind tended to race. He was upset that he could not get control over his health, and this caused him to feel increasingly more irritable and depressed. He added that he often felt anxious and used food for "comfort."

Eric was married and had two children. He loved his family and spending time with them. One of the activities they did together regularly was to attend services at a nondenominational church. He added that though he found solace in prayer and meditation, he was not sure how he truly felt about God, but it brought the family together. His oldest son was leaving for college soon, and although he was excited for his son, he was also anxious and sad to see him go. In addition, he loathed his job. He stayed because of the financial benefits, since his real occupation of being an artist and writer could not support a family. He was rarely able to do his artwork.

Eric had grown up in a large Catholic family who lived in a small house, the third child of nine. His parents were "good" people who took their religion very seriously. They were not forthcoming with emotions or with loving touch. The family life was entrenched in Catholicism. All the children went to Catholic school, and he and his brothers were altar boys. He trusted and believed everything he was told by his parents, his teachers, and the Church. He obeyed, did what he was told, and followed the rules. He believed that he was being "watched" and that if he wasn't good, he would be punished by the nuns, his parents, or God himself. He recalled being reprimanded on many occasions and constantly feeling ashamed, guilty, or fearful. He never felt that anything he did was good enough.

Eric went on to explain that when he went away to college, he rebelled against his upbringing. He took up transcendental meditation, as it provided him structure and helped him clear his mind of thoughts. He later moved away from transcendental meditation, finding that the movement had become too rigid and had too many rules, which reminded him too much of his Catholic upbringing. He did not return to meditation or prayer until he was married and joined the nondenominational church with his wife. This, he stated, he had done mostly to provide another way to keep his family together. If it weren't for them, he wouldn't go.

As with most of my patients, the first step for Eric was building trust and healing his heart.

I worked with Eric on creating a SHIELD and opening his heart. His first positive verbal command was "I trust that I am loved and supported." I taught Eric to use the imagery of the divine parents, standing in the SHIELD and providing him with love and support. We also devised a health plan that would include better self-care strategies, such as improved sleep, hygiene, and exercise and nutrition plans.

By his next visit, Eric reported that he was sleeping better, his back pain had lessened, and he was feeling slightly more centered. His blood pressure was still high, however, and he still often felt irritable and depressed. He was experiencing job stress, which took up a lot of his energy. He also noticed that a lot of anger had been coming to the surface of late, and it was not just related to work. The angrier he became, the less he exercised and the poorer food choices he made.

He thought that it might have something to do with the recent scandals associated with the Catholic Church. He felt upset, devastated, and angry. Even though he had never been sexually abused as a child, he felt violated, betrayed, and had a profound sense of loss and sorrow. It seemed that everything he had been taught as a child was made up of lies. How could he trust anymore?

Why, I asked, did his anger cause him to practice self-destruction rather than self-care, when he was claiming to be angry at the Church? Perhaps, I told him, we needed to examine his feelings of anger and loss.

I asked Eric to close his eyes, to think about the Church and, when he did, if he experienced any discomfort in the body, to tell me where. Eric said he experienced a constricted feeling in his chest. When I asked him to ask the constriction why it was there, he answered, "I am here because I am sad. I feel alienated. I feel deserted by God. I feel betrayed by the people who were supposed to be doing good things. I am angry at these people who misinterpreted God to me and at God for letting them. I feel alone and lonely."

"And how do you feel about yourself?" I asked. He answered, "I feel ashamed. I feel responsible. I should have known. I must have done something wrong to make this happen." He then cried. His body shook as he cried out and tears streamed down his face.

I guided Eric through the Child of Perfection healing. He imagined seeing himself at the age of seven and embracing that child. He imagined the two of them surrounded by the SHIELD of divine light and repeated to himself that they were both loved and never alone. He then imagined the two of them running, playing, laughing, singing, or doing whatever he felt would bring joy and innocence back to his heart.

I asked Eric to do this exercise daily for the next month, to enable him to be in better touch with his emotions, face his anger, release it, heal his heart, and start the process of forgiveness, mostly of forgiving himself. His homework was to practice connecting with the imagery of the divine light, to remember that there was something that was larger than him that also offered him support and love rather than hardship and pain.

By the following month, Eric's blood pressure readings were finally coming down. He felt less angry and resentful. Still, he felt a tremendous sense of loss and that his life lacked meaning, especially since his children were leaving home.

Eric needed to fill up his Love Reserves more in order to feel whole and complete and better able to let go of his children.

I taught him the Connecting to Heaven and Earth healing visualization (which you will learn shortly). I also asked him to keep an Appreciation Journal to reinforce his sense of gratitude for all that he had and all that he was, rather than what he was losing.

On his last visit, Eric happily reported that he was doing better. He had been practicing the reprogramming tools daily, writing a lot in his Appreciation Journal, and writing short stories. He had been spending more time walking outdoors. His blood pressure was down to normal. He felt calmer overall and was starting to contemplate what else he might do for work. He did not feel an urgency to make the change, though, since he felt more grounded. He still was sad that his children were grown and leaving, but he also felt that he would have the resources to handle the change. He felt optimistic rather than fearful about discovering what was next in his path, because he knew now his life had meaning.

Goal 3: Face and heal the wounds that are the source of your suffering.

Your Love Rx for Relaxing into Love

AWARENESS EXERCISE

Part 1: Awareness of Your Faith

This awareness exercise centers around the notion of God, and it may seem controversial to some. Why am I asking you to do this? Most of you were likely raised with a certain understanding of what or who God is. You might have grown up with a set of rules and were told that you were "bad" if you did not obey them and that you would be punished, just like Eric. This might have led to many negative associations with religion, whether you are aware of them now or not. God became a punishing God. So even though, as adults, you may be "spiritual," your unconscious mind still carries old information relating to this belief system. My goal is for you to rid yourself of the unconscious assumption that the universe is punishing you if and when something goes wrong. I want you to see that the word "God" can be just that, a word, and the universe, just like you, is loving and helpful.

I am not telling you to believe. I cannot give you scientific proof that a higher being or an ever-present goodness exists. I am telling you that you can choose whether or not you want to believe. I am also suggesting that if you choose to believe, you will feel better.

Try it and see what happens.

Set a timer for ten minutes.
Close your eyes.
Inhale deeply.
Exhale completely.
Create your SHIELD.
Ask your heart to show you how you really feel about the idea of God.
What is your attitude toward the concept of God?
What are your expectations of God?
How has God failed you or helped you?
Notice the sensations in your chest.
Notice the thoughts, emotions, and feelings that come up.
Do you feel connected to a higher power or not?
Does your heart feel open to the connection or closed?
If it feels closed, where do you feel it in your chest?
Examine the spot or spots in your chest that feel closed.
Ask those spots to show you what is in there.
What are the experiences or what is the information that the heart is basing its reaction on?
Why did your heart close down to protect itself?
What happened to you?
Did something happen to you when you were younger that caused you to lose trust?
When did you let go of your idea that something else existed other than just you and the world you could see, hear, or feel?
Allow images, thoughts, emotions, and feelings to rise up.
Observe without judging or holding back.

Part 2: The Release

Reset the timer for fifteen minutes.

1. Whatever your experience, it is neither right nor wrong. It is your experience, and it is valid. When you are done with the awareness exercise, write down your experience. Write without stopping. Whatever you write does not even need to make sense. Just write.
2. When the timer goes off, place your hands on the words and say, "I now release you from my body." Then destroy the paper. Follow this exercise with Part 3: Connecting to Heaven and Earth.

Goal 4: Heal by connecting to Heaven and Earth.

Part 3: The Healing: Connecting to Heaven and Earth

Close your eyes.
Inhale deeply.
Exhale completely.
Create your SHIELD.
The divine parents are standing in your SHIELD, holding
    you and comforting you.
Imagine you are standing at the peak of a mountain.
You are barefoot.
You feel the earth beneath your feet.
Feel your feet grounded in the earth, supported and held, as
    if your feet have roots that go deep into the earth.
From deep within the earth, the earth feeds you abundance,
    love, and nurturance.
Allow yourself to receive the love and support through your
    roots from the earth.
Spend some time acknowledging and appreciating this
    connection.
Shift your awareness to the sun shining down upon you
    from the sky above.
It is shining down upon you like a shower of light.
Notice how soothing and loving the light feels as it warms
    the crown of your head.
The ray of sun touching the crown of your head is like a
    rope made up of light coming from the heavens above.

You are directly connected to the heavens above through this
    rope of light.
The heavens are feeding you with abundance, love, and
    nurturance.
Allow yourself to receive the love and support through the
    rope of light from the heavens.
Spend some time acknowledging and appreciating your
    connection to the heavens.
You are connected to Heaven and Earth.
You are connected to all things.
Anything is possible for you.
You do not need to hold yourself up.
Surrender into your connection to Heaven and Earth, which
    holds you and supports you.
Trust that you are loved and supported.
Say to yourself, "I trust that I am loved and supported."
Relax into love as you fall back into your SHIELD of light.
Relax into love.
Do this as long as you wish.

Daily Reprogramming Tools for Relaxing into Love

Once you have established the "relax into love" experience in your
memory, you may find that when you utter those words throughout
your day, your body feels more relaxed and your emotions calm down
instantaneously.

WHAT TO DO
- Create the SHIELD.
- Repeat the positive verbal commands "I trust that I am loved
  and supported" and "relax into love," as you imagine that you
  are doing the "Spiritual Trust fall" into your SHIELD of divine
  light.
- Say the Heart Prayer and the Trust Prayer.
- Practice self-care behaviors such as improving your nutrition,
  getting enough sleep, and exercising.
- Practice the Love Radar and the Child of Perfection to Infinity
  Healing.

- Spend some time writing in your Appreciation Journal.
- Spend more time out in nature.
- Connect to the earth and to the heavens with the Connecting to Heaven and Earth healing visualization.

WHEN TO USE THE REPROGRAMMING TOOLS
- When you feel overwhelmed by your circumstance or uncertainty.
- When you feel alone and isolated.
- When you feel anxious or depressed.
- When you feel that someone or something is to blame for why your life has gone wrong.
- When you are in physical, emotional, or psychological pain and nothing helps.
- When nothing you do seems to help anything—your work, your health, your home, your relationships, etc.
- When you cannot sleep.

When you learn to trust and surrender to something divine, you connect with the larger world, to the universe, space, and Spirit. You connect to wisdom, spiritual connection, and a sense of peace and oneness with all that exists. You feel part of a larger whole, and you feel complete without needing someone else to complete you. You use faith as well as your intellect or rational analysis to work through the things you do not understand.

You begin to accept all beings, including yourself, recognizing that we are all part of this larger whole. You learn to love unconditionally, embracing all that is, through scars and imperfections. You can then communicate this love freely and openly to all living things and put Spiritual Love into action, spreading your light through the world for all to see.

13

SPIRITUAL LOVE IN ACTION

D.I.G. (Dignity, Integrity, and Grace)

Practicing Spiritual Love creates in you a knowledge that the universe, the earth, or some higher being supports and loves you and that you are connected to all beings and all things. With this knowledge, you understand that who you are affects who others are and will be; that as you heal, you heal others; as you grow, you enable others to grow. As your heart is "tickled," you tickle someone else's heart.

You do it because you want to and you do it because you can. This is Spiritual Love in action.

Your last mission toward completing the Spiritual Love side of your Love Pyramid is to achieve these six goals:

1. Know that you are not alone.
2. Honor yourself, others, and the environment.
3. Connect with the needs of others through empathy.
4. Live your life with dignity, integrity, and grace.
5. Help others heal their wounds through altruistic love.
6. Learn that you are not separate but connected to all things and have available to you all that you need to mitigate uncertainty.

Goal 1: Know that you are not alone.

United We Stand

I don't think anyone can forget the events of September 11, 2001, when the whole world sat glued to the television, watching the towers of New York's World Trade Center go up in flames and implode into clouds of billowing smoke, over and over again. Horror and shock set in as we watched the devastation. We moved through emotions of shock, grief, anger, and despair. We felt helpless, and many of us did whatever we could to try to help—whether it was giving blood, going to ground zero and offering our services, or simply being nice to one another. Do you remember how civil people were with one another? I remember that here in Boston, road rage vanished. People said "Please" and "Thank you." They made room for one another. The sense of a unified front prevailed, of banding together for a just cause. This incredible atrocity had done one amazing feat—it brought people together who might never have otherwise spoken to one another.

We all felt the pain. We knew that our pain was shared. We were not alone. And this gave us strength. Our united front empowered us.

Eventually, of course, life resumed to normal, especially for those not so closely affected by that dark day's tragic events. People went back into the cocoons of their own lives. If anything, the atrocities of 9/11 and the ensuing "war on terror" worked to further activate our nation's Fear Response, adding to the already existing feelings of fear and anger that come with life in modern America. That sense of unity and togetherness seemed to dissolve, as most people had to turn their attention back to the pressing needs in their lives.

Why did this happen?

Because most people were running on empty and still had needs waiting to be met, no matter how much they grieved and wanted to reach out to help.

Most people do not have sufficient resources to help them feel strong and whole so that they can help without losing their balance, at least not for an extended period of time. And when they are not involved in a larger purpose and are only dealing with their everyday fears and problems, they often feel separate and alone.

When you fill up your Love Reserves so that love is overflowing, you have ample ability to share this love with others, simply by honoring them, and to manage your own problems simultaneously.

Learning D.I.G. (Dignity, Integrity, and Grace)

I was driving to work one day, wrapped up in my own thoughts, when the traffic suddenly slowed to a halt. Initially I was furious, angry that I was going to be late. When I pulled myself out of my thoughts, I saw that the holdup was for a funeral procession. Indignant, I complained, "Oh, no! This is going to take forever!" I looked to my left, and I saw six firemen lined up outside the firehouse, saluting. I remembered that I had heard on the news that several firemen had died in a recent fire and one of them was from my area.

When I realized that this must have been one of the fallen firemen's funeral procession, I was instantaneously flooded with profound sadness, mixed with guilt for my resentful thoughts and behavior. My chest hurt, and tears rolled down my face. "Why?" I thought guiltily, once the traffic started moving again. "Why did I go from feeling entitled and angry to feeling such sorrow and grief when I saw the firemen standing there? Why didn't I feel that way when I thought it was the funeral of a civilian? Am I such an unfeeling jerk that I couldn't pull myself out of my thoughts for another person and their bereaved family? Or am I just so wrapped up in myself that it isn't until something that is related to me happens that I take notice? How was the fireman's funeral related to me anyway? I didn't know him personally."

Rather than trying to work through the answers right away, I created my SHIELD first, because I knew that my reaction resulted from the triggering of one of my wounds.

Surrounded by divine light, feeling calm and at peace, I examined first why I felt such a tremendous sense of loss. I noted that I felt grief over the loss of something or someone honorable and noble. That fireman had lost his life for me, indirectly. He and others like him had signed up to serve and protect me, so that I could live my life believing I could be safe. What did the image of the fireman represent for me? I asked myself. The image stood for courage in the face of the unknown and being able to live one's life in service, with dignity, integrity, and grace. Had I in any way sacrificed my life for this person and his family? Had I done anything honorable and noble? Indeed, my indignant behavior was hardly dignified or full of integrity. Perhaps this was my opportunity to pull myself out of my small world of putting so much importance on getting to work on time and reconnecting to the larger world. Perhaps this was a chance for me to heal my wound of loss so that I could feel complete and whole.

Rather than getting angry with myself for my poor behavior, I honored my feelings for signaling that I was out of balance. I repeated my Trust Prayer and allowed myself to be comforted by the divine light and love. When I felt a sense of calm and peace, I extended my love and prayers to the firemen who had perished, to their families, and to all others who might be feeling what I was feeling. I set an intention to live my life with dignity, integrity, and grace every day. In my everyday actions I could be a representative of what it was these men stood for.

Within minutes, I found I was less in a rush about getting to work. I acted more kindly to my fellow drivers and coworkers. I paid more attention to the food choices I made that day, honoring my body. I listened more carefully to my patients, honoring their experiences. I picked up litter that I saw flying around outside the supermarket, honoring my environment. And when I found, every so often, that my Fear Response was activated, I created my SHIELD and said to myself, "D.I.G.: dignity, integrity, grace," and immediately felt my physiology shift from negativity to positivity.

To D.I.G. is to honor. This is why the second letter in "SHIELD" stands for "honor." When you learn to honor yourself, your feelings, your body, and your experiences, you can learn to honor all else that is around you. By honoring, you create an immediate connection and sense of appreciation between you and the object, person, or place. You make yourself, the object, person, or place important and valuable, which is what everyone ultimately wants to feel.

Goal 2: Honor yourself, others, and the environment.

YOUR TURN: PRACTICE HONORING

You can practice honoring in everything that you do and everywhere you go. You can make statements during everyday activities such as:

- I honor this food that I eat.
- I honor the farmer who grew these vegetables.

- I honor the individual who made these clothes.
- I honor my body with the foods I give it.
- I honor my body and offer it rest when it needs it.
- I honor the postman who has delivered my mail.

You also can create a sacred space in your home or workplace. It can be a place where you worship or meditate or simply are quiet. When you step over the threshold, put aside all negativity, complaints, and misery. Here, you only honor. I recommend spending ten to twenty minutes each day contemplating honoring yourself—all that you are, all that you have overcome, and all that you have accomplished. Then repeat these words to yourself:

Dignity
Integrity
Grace
Notice how you feel.

Goal 3: Connect to the needs of others through empathy.

DEVELOPING EMPATHY

Honoring other people enables you to have empathy for them, meaning you can better understand and appreciate them. You have the ability to communicate with them, as you are able to view yourself and the world through their eyes. Of course, it is difficult to honor and communicate when you feel bad. When you feel bad, it is hard to be kind to your environment. So, as I did, you may want to heal yourself first, noticing your own negative emotions, feelings, or reactions and then trying to understand why they are there. When you understand your own pain, you are more likely to be able to examine someone else's beliefs and circumstances, enabling you to better understand, honor, and appreciate what they need.

I am sure most of you have experienced walking into a room full of tension and immediately wanting to leave. Nothing was said to you and no harm was done to you, but you still wanted to leave because of the discomfort you felt by being in the very tense environment. In this same way, by paying attention to the sensations in your body, you can pick up when another person is in distress, without that person needing to say a word.

By paying attention to the sensations in your body, especially your heart, you can connect with the pervasive emotions that most people also are experiencing. You can connect to the collective experience.

The problem is that most people cannot separate their own discomfort from other people's. In order to do so, you have to work on alleviating your own suffering first so that you can increase the size of your cushion of love and have enough reserves to help someone else.

JOLIE: *Finding Her Heart and Discovering Empathy*

Jolie, thirty-eight years old, was concerned about her immune system. She had just gotten over a bout of pneumonia and a recurrent strep throat. She complained of gaining twenty pounds in the past year and having low energy. She denied eating a lot and reported that even when she trained for a triathlon, she still gained weight. She complained of frequent asthma attacks and allergies to her environment, and now it seemed she was also forming food allergies. Her body also ached, which she attributed to her long hours of training for the triathlon.

Jolie denied feeling depressed or anxious. She did not feel "stressed." Rather, she felt frustrated that she could not control her body. She felt, psychologically and emotionally, "fine." In fact, anytime I asked Jolie how something made her feel emotionally, she answered, "Fine. It doesn't bother me at all." I got the same answer even when I asked about how she felt about her mother's constant bouts with depression or her recent breakup with her boyfriend.

The oldest of three children, Jolie had grown up in a loving home, though no one really demonstrated their love through touch or hugs. They were well provided for and spent a lot of family time together. Her mother suffered from major depression that became mostly permanent when Jolie was in high school.

To test out my suspicion, I led Jolie through the Opening the Heart healing visualization. Although she felt rested and more relaxed after the exercise, Jolie exclaimed, "I have no heart!" She explained that her heart was dark. It never took in the divine light and instead remained empty and dark. She felt nothing.

I explained to Jolie that she did indeed have a heart, as she was living and breathing, but that her heart had created so much armor around it that she was closed off from connecting with herself and just as likely from connecting to others. The end of her relationship with her boyfriend might have affected her more than she realized, and it might have triggered old wounds from her childhood, perhaps related to her mother's withdrawal when Jolie was a teenager. Her body was shutting down and shutting out, the muscles were constricted, her metabolism was slow, and her weight was not coming off.

It was time for Jolie to allow her repressed feelings to emerge. We had to create a cushion of love for her so that she would not feel so vulnerable.

I sent her home with instructions to practice becoming aware of her body's signals, to notice if emotions came up and to allow them to do so, rather than repressing them, and to keep an Awareness Journal. She was also to keep an Appreciation Journal and practice honoring her body, her feelings, and herself. Jolie was also to practice the SHIELD and the Heart Prayer along with the Opening the Heart healing visualization. We discussed a modified nutrition plan, sleep, hygiene, and exercise program that would not overtax her immune system but help it recuperate and get stronger. Her positive verbal command was "I trust that I am loved and supported."

Over the next three months, Jolie began to feel better. Her energy level improved, her allergies were less active, she slept better, and her body felt less tense. She still felt frustrated that her weight had not changed and she was easily irritated. She admitted she was stressed because her mother had been diagnosed with lung cancer. She had little time to be upset about it because of problems at work. She could not face her mother's illness. As painful as it was, I explained to Jolie that she was going to have to face it and that she might need to allow herself to fall apart. I reassured her that she could fall apart because her cushion of love would break her fall.

I guided Jolie through the Opening the Heart healing visualization again. This time, she was able to see her heart light up partially. She complained of feeling a pain in her chest that radiated through to the back. She also began to cry, tears that she had not allowed herself to shed for a long, long time.

I asked Jolie to close her eyes and look into the painful feeling in her chest. She reported that she felt a big knot, like a sailor's knot, in her left upper chest and back. She said it felt as if a fist had been shoved into that area. The pain felt angry, as if it did not want her there, and it was threatening to radiate all through her body if she came any closer. It was telling her that if she loosened up the rest of her body or emotions, the pain would spread.

I led Jolie through the visualization of the SHIELD and the divine parents in order to create a cushion for her that she was indeed loved and supported so that she would not be scared of this pain. I then guided her back into the painful area, to look more deeply into this wound.

ME: "You are in the wound, what do you see?"
JOLIE: "I see a little girl, feeling alone and scared, but she has to be strong because Mommy is feeling sad."
ME: "Why does she have to be strong?"
JOLIE: "If she is strong and happy, Mommy will get better."
ME: "Is it helping? Is Mommy getting better?"
JOLIE: "No. It is not working."
ME: "How is it making her feel?"
JOLIE: "Angry. No matter what she does, Mommy does not get better."

I invited the divine mother into the visualization to comfort the image of Jolie's little girl and to let her know that her mother's pain was not her fault and not her responsibility to cure; that just because Jolie felt her mother's pain it didn't mean she had to heal it. It was not her fault that her mother was sick. Her only responsibility was to love herself so that she could continue to love her mother. I asked Jolie to repeat the Trust Prayer.

The pain in Jolie's upper back started to dissipate as she allowed herself to be filled with love and support. I asked her to say to herself, "D.I.G."—dignity, integrity, grace—so that she could feel whole and complete. Then she was to extend love and support to her mother. By the end of the meditation, Jolie exclaimed, "I have a heart! It's full of light and wide open! I have a heart!"

These visualizations and reprogramming exercises helped Jolie manage over the next six months, until her mother's death. Despite the difficulties, she persisted in practicing self-care strategies, repeating her positive verbal commands and visualizations. As she began to honor herself and her life, she felt she wanted to become closer to a spiritual community. She became more active in her church and spent more time with friends whom she didn't have to be strong and happy for all the time. She allowed herself to feel and to heal, so that she could be with her mother fully until her death. And even though she grieved, she felt at peace. She also felt a deep sense of gratitude for all that she had and all the love that she had received. Now she wanted to share it.

Jolie went on spiritual retreats and became more active in her community, reaching out to those in need and volunteering her time.

The more she gave, the bigger her heart felt and the stronger she became both physically and emotionally.

At a recent visit she asked me why she felt sad and experienced chest pain when one of the women in her women's group was talking about her troubles or occasionally during the priest's sermon. She was confused because she, Jolie, was not upset about anything in particular at the time. I asked her if there was a common theme that both the woman and priest spoke about. Jolie noted that both the priest and the woman spoke about loss. I explained then that she, Jolie, was experiencing empathy.

Jolie had experienced loss herself, so hearing others speak about loss touched her own wound. Because she had done so much healing already, she was able to observe her physical pain, rather than become consumed by it. In observing her pain, she could then discern that her pain was the same pain someone else was feeling too.

Your Love Rx for Empathy

AWARENESS EXERCISE

Part 1: Awareness of Empathy

You can do this exercise alone or with a partner. If you work with a partner, both of you should write out, in a sentence or two, about a situation that has been upsetting to you. The other person will be reading it. If you are alone, think about a traumatic situation, either one you have seen on television, a historical event, or something you have heard about recently. Perhaps someone has been hurt or killed; some family has lost their son or daughter; someone has had to go through a divorce or breakup.

> Set a timer for ten minutes.
> Close your eyes.
> Inhale deeply.
> Exhale completely.
> Create your SHIELD.
> Think about the situation; think about the other people or person involved.
> See them clearly.

What are you feeling?

What sensations do you notice in your chest?

What is happening with your breath?

Allow images to come up for you.

Do not be frightened.

You are safe.

Look deeper.

Observe what you see and feel.

When the timer goes off, stop.

Part 2: The Release

Reset the timer for fifteen minutes.

1. Write down whatever you have felt or are feeling and whatever you saw or experienced. You may draw instead of writing if you wish, or do this as well as writing.
2. Draw your pain, what you are feeling or experiencing.
3. When you are done, place your hands on the words and say, "I now release you from my body." Then destroy the paper.
4. If you are working with a partner, place your hand on each other's heart and say out loud, "I hear you." Then take turns talking about your experience.

    Follow this exercise with Part 3: D.I.G.

Goal 4: Live your life with dignity, integrity, and grace.

Part 3: The Healing: D.I.G. (Dignity, Integrity, and Grace)

Close your eyes.

Inhale deeply.

Exhale completely.

Create your SHIELD.

Your SHIELD of divine light is shining down upon you.

You are immersed in unconditional love and light.

Command your Love Radar to appear by saying "Radar!" silently to yourself.

The radar of divine light will begin to spin and shine in your

heart center, calling out for love, bringing in love to your
heart, and transmitting out love to the outside world.

Fill your heart with love and light and then extend it out to
your partner or the person or situation that you were
thinking about.

Call out to the heavens for help by saying "Calling all love
from the Heavens!"

As you do so, the divine light and love from the heavens
shine down through the crown of your head, down into
the center of your Love Radar in your heart.

Call to the earth for help by saying "Calling all love from
the earth!"

The earth will send divine light and love up through the
earth into your feet, up through your body, into your
Love Radar.

Continue to transmit love and light through your Love
Radar out to the world or others.

Transmit love and light to the people or person from your
awareness exercise.

You are an open vessel of love and light, receiving and giving.

You are a "love conductor."

And you are filled with dignity, integrity, and grace.

Say these words: "Dignity, integrity, and grace."

Daily Reprogramming Tools for Achieving Dignity, Integrity, and Grace

WHAT TO DO

- Create your SHIELD.
- Surround yourself with divine light and love.
- Surrender into your SHIELD.
- Create the Love Radar by calling out your demand: "Radar!"
- Create your Love Conductor by calling out for help from the
  Heavens and the Earth, then extend the light and love
  anywhere that you wish.
- Say, "D.I.G." or "Dignity, integrity, grace." (You can say these
  words anytime you need to, with or without the SHIELD in
  place.)

- Practice random acts of kindness—at least once a day—for yourself and for others.
- Make an effort to say thank you, recognizing and appreciating the efforts of others.
- Practice appreciating the beauty and wonder of nature.
- Practice appreciating how things are made that you normally take for granted—the food you eat, the chair you sit on, or the car you drive—so that you can practice being in awe.
- Keep an Appreciation Journal.

WHEN TO USE THE REPROGRAMMING TOOLS
- Anytime you are feeling disconnected from others or yourself.
- Anytime you are having a hard time understanding someone else or their actions.
- Anytime you feel overwhelmed by the world around you, not understanding why bad things have happened to good people.
- Anytime you see that someone else is in need.
- Anytime you disapprove of someone else's behavior or actions and find yourself judging them.
- When you lack appreciation of yourself and the world around you.
- When you are mistreating your environment or someone else or see someone else doing the same.
- When you have negative feelings, thoughts, actions, or emotions about certain people or certain situations (this usually implies that the person or situation is in trouble too).

Goal 5: Help others heal their wounds through altruistic love.

FROM EMPATHY TO ALTRUISM AND FROM I TO WE: THE TICKLE EFFECT

When you fully establish your Love Pyramid, you may discover that you want to share your love with the world. You understand that you will not lose yourself in other people or material things, so you can easily connect to and commit to the larger whole. You can live in a constant state of love, so that when you see or experience suffering, your cushion of love helps you maintain your balance. You understand others' suffering. You do not react in the Fear Response, but you shift into the Love Response, remaining calm, seeing clearly, finding meaning, and ultimately achieving wisdom. Despite having witnessed all this suffering, you still smile and laugh. You still love fully because your heart has softened. You feel safe because you are no longer just an "I" but a "we." You are not alone.

When your heart softens, you can be wise, but you can also be playful and full of joy, like a child with a wide-open heart. You can embrace life with abandonment, with laugh-out-loud spontaneity and joy. You become ticklish again, just as you were as a child.

Difficult life experiences, disappointments, and hurts often close the heart. Then we stop being ticklish. Softening our heart as an adult, as you have learned, involves healing the past events that caused the heart to close in the first place. It involves opening our mind so that we can really see and think clearly. Once we achieve this, we can be both wise and childlike. We can be serious without taking ourselves so seriously. We can be tickled into laughter again, even though life can be difficult.

When our heart softens, we practice random acts of kindness toward ourselves, others, and our environment. We find that we have more appreciation and awe of the world and more empathy. In our acts of kindness we tickle someone else's heart, so they too can be wise and also childlike. We add to someone else's Love Reserves so that they just might tickle someone else's heart and so on, so that at the end, we have instigated the Tickle Effect. Then, all of a sudden, we realize that we do not feel so separate from the world but *one* with it.

I believe that most people crave a sense of oneness, awe, and unconditional love in life. I also know that when you believe you are alone and separated from your resources, you are in stress and will activate your Fear Response. When you believe you are connected to yourself, others, or nature or the universe, when you know you are part of a "we" instead of just an "I," you activate the Love Response.

THE SINAI DESERT AND ONE BIG TICKLE EFFECT

Two years after 9/11, I went to Israel to celebrate my friend Elina's birthday. The plan was for ten of us to travel to the Sinai Desert in Egypt for a week's time. We were excited, as there is no place in the world quite like the Sinai, with its vast expanses of sand, rolling mountains, star-filled skies, and the clear blue waters of the Red Sea. In the Sinai, for all of us, it felt as if time stood still. There, the rhythm of our everyday life no longer existed and we became attuned only to the rhythm of nature. We all knew that going there would be our chance to escape the stress of our everyday lives, to feel the sense of oneness with nature and with one another, to celebrate our dear friend's life. We intended to go to a place called Devil's Head.

When I arrived in Israel, Elina decided to postpone our trip for a few days since she was appearing on television and wanted to see the show. The day that we were meant to be in the Sinai, we found ourselves still in Tel Aviv, going to a different party to pass the time before Elina's television show would be on. No sooner did we arrive at the party than cell phones began to ring. "Oh my god!" were the sounds everywhere. The Sinai had been bombed. It seemed that everyone at the party knew someone who had traveled there because it was the Jewish New Year, when many Israelis travel to the Sinai. The level of tension and worry rose in the house so that it was palpable. In no time, the people in the house began to comfort one another and share information. We sat glued to the TV, waiting to see what was happening and how many casualties there would be.

For a long time, no one knew what had happened and how many people had been injured. Israeli ambulances could not get across the border. Most travelers were somewhere in the middle of the desert, without running electricity or phone lines. We were tense and worried. I also remember feeling something else—an unspoken bond among everyone in the nation. It was palpable.

Soon the news reported that the bombs had landed in three places and one of those places was Devil's Head. We were in shock. It could have been us there. We could have been there, injured, dead, or simply scared out of our minds.

We hugged one another and cried. Not only could it have been us, but we knew people who were there. It would be some time before we would know if they were okay. We didn't much feel like celebrating.

After some deliberation, we understood that we had two options. We could close our hearts and stay angry, worried, and scared. Or we could soften our hearts, celebrate our lives, and honor the lives of others. We could celebrate and honor our love for one another and our country, and especially for our dear friend Elina.

We celebrated and had a magical evening. We shared an experience together that bonded us more than before. The evening was filled with laughter and love. At one point I remember Elina saying "Look at this. We brought the Sinai here." It was true. We had planned to go to the Sinai because it was the one place in the world where we felt part of a much larger whole, a place where we felt we had all we needed. And now we had that through the love we shared for one another. We had brought Spiritual Love into our midst. We had created one big tickle effect that helped us handle the traumatic bombing of a place we held sacred and pure, and of the people we honored and loved. We could handle the pain of what had happened and still connect to joy.

Goal 6: Learn that you are not separate but connected to all things and have available to you all that you need to mitigate uncertainty.

Your Love Rx for the Tickle Effect

Awareness Exercise

Part 1: Awareness of Separateness

> Set a timer for ten minutes.
> Close your eyes.
> Breathe in deeply.
> Exhale completely.
> Create your SHIELD.
> You are safe in your SHIELD.
> Relax into your body.
> Start to pay attention to sensations in your body.
> You are standing alone in a jungle.
> No one is there but you and foraging animals.
> You are lost.
> You have no connection to anyone or anything.
> You are in the middle of nowhere. All alone.
> You are about out of water and food.
> You do not know where to turn.
> You do not know which way to go.
> You are lost.
> What do you feel.
> Notice the fear rise up in your body.
> Notice the sensations.

Notice the thoughts.

Notice the emotions.

Observe what you feel and what images come up for you.

What do you see yourself doing and feeling?

Have you had these sensations, thoughts, or feelings before?

If so, when?

Let the past experience or image come up for you when you
  felt this way before.

When the timer goes off, stop.

Part 2: The Release

Reset the timer for fifteen minutes.

1. Begin to write about your experience. As before, do not hold
   back and let the words flow out. Write down your fears and
   experience of being alone and separated from all things, including life itself. What was it like?
2. When the timer goes off, place your hands on the words
   and say, "I now release you from my body." Then destroy the
   paper.

Follow this exercise with Part 3: We Have All That We Need.

Part 3: The Healing: We Have All That We Need

Close your eyes.

Inhale deeply.

Exhale completely.

Create your SHIELD.

Every time you exhale, your breath sweeps away tension,
  stress, and negativity from your mind and body.

Now bring your attention and your awareness to the center
  of your chest, the part of it known as the heart center.

Relax into your heart center.

Now imagine, in your heart center, the face of a person you
  love.

See his or her face clearly.

See him or her smiling at you lovingly, looking at you with loving eyes.

Remember what it feels like to be looked at by eyes that love you in such a way.

Remember what it feels like to be with this person whom you love so much and who loves you.

Smile back at that person lovingly.

Look at him or her with loving eyes.

Embrace him or her.

Say these words silently to yourself: "Our hearts are one heart, we have all that we need." "Our hearts are one heart, we have all that we need." "Our hearts are one heart, we have all that we need."

As your heart opens, your hearts begin to merge together into one heart.

Keep repeating these words: "Our hearts are one heart, we have all that we need."

Your merged hearts become even larger, beginning to merge with everyone in your building, so that your heart is the center of the building.

Keep repeating these words: "Our hearts are one heart, we have all that we need."

Your merged hearts become even larger, beginning to merge with everyone in your city, so that your heart is the center of the city.

Keep repeating these words: "Our hearts are one heart, we have all that we need."

Your merged hearts become even larger, beginning to merge with everyone in your country, so that your heart is the center of the country.

Keep repeating these words: "Our hearts are one heart, we have all that we need."

Your merged hearts become even larger, beginning to merge with everyone on the earth, so that your heart is the center of the earth.

Keep repeating these words: "Our hearts are one heart, we have all that we need."

Your merged hearts become even larger, beginning to merge

with everyone in the universe, so that your heart is the
center of the universe.

Keep repeating these words: "Our hearts are one heart, we
have all that we need."

You can intentionally extend your heart to anyone or
anywhere that you wish.

You can send it to yourself, to someone you love, to
someone you need to forgive, or to someone who needs to
forgive you.

Send this love to someone alive or now gone.

Send this love to one person or as many living beings as you
wish.

Take all the time you need.

Keep repeating these words: "Our hearts are one heart, we
have all that we need."

Daily Reprogramming Tools for Building Spiritual Love

WHAT TO DO

- Create your SHIELD.
- Surround yourself with loving and healing light.
- Imagine a person you love sitting in your heart.
- Say the positive verbal command "Our hearts are one heart. We
  have all that we need."
- Make an effort to connect with those you love.
- Make an effort to connect with nature and your environment.
- Make an effort to talk about your fears so that you can release
  them and better receive the help that is available to you.

WHEN TO USE THE REPROGRAMMING TOOLS

- Anytime you feel alone or scared.
- Anytime you question whether you are enough or have
  enough—whether money, education, time, or resources.
- Anytime you feel worried about what might happen to our
  planet or to our world.
- Anytime you watch the TV news.
- Anytime you feel bad about someone else's situation and feel
  helpless about helping them.

- Anytime you feel bad about your own situation and feel helpless.
- Anytime you feel separated from people, especially from the people you love.

It is possible to develop a sense of oneness with all things and achieve a big Tickle Effect without going anywhere or being someone different from who you are now. All it takes is developing Social Love, which allows you to develop Self-Love, which then allows you to fully connect with Spiritual Love. With your Love Pyramid intact, you will know that you have all that you need. When you know you have all that you need, you will rush to share love with the rest of the world.

Ultimately, the less you live in your Fear Response, the better you feel. When you feel good, you are more likely to be altruistic and compassionate toward others. Invariably, you then feel better about yourself, perpetuating a cycle of living in your Love Response. As a result, your physiology changes, reprogrammed from negative to positive, and you find you are happier and healthier.

EPILOGUE

COME SWIM WITH ME

Love is the secret to your health and well-being. Each and every patient who walks through my door is offered a space where they can be loved; a space where they can be seen, heard, and validated; a space where they can learn to love themselves, learn to receive love from others, and learn to connect to something larger than themselves. They learn how to create a Love Pyramid, made up of Social Love, Self-Love, and Spiritual Love. They then may discover that they are whole and have their own natural abilities to heal. They learn to open and soften their hearts and, in so doing, find new ways to see the world and operate in it.

Many wisdom traditions hold the belief that when the heart softens and you feel whole, you experience feelings of oneness and universal connection. You experience spiritual wisdom and many other desirable qualities: balance, acceptance, self-knowledge, the gift of intuitive vision and clarity, openness to spiritual experience, strong powers of the mind and will, and feelings of connectedness and purpose. You also tap into the potential for profound healing and restructuring of body and mind, so that you are able to transcend time and space and experience enlightenment.

I think enlightenment has been given a bad rap of sorts. It is often touted as unattainable by the ordinary person. To me, enlightenment simply refers to connecting with and loving your true self, connecting with and loving the true self of others, and connecting to Spiritual

Love, knowing that we are all divine beings. Enlightenment means you gain intuition, wisdom, and the ability to see the entire picture—the good and the bad, the light and the dark, the ups and the downs. You do not get stuck in rigid patterns or in one thought or idea. You are open to new ideas and points of view. You are awake and aware, and can experience things that are not necessarily visible to the physical eye, heard by the ear, or felt by the hand. You also have an enormous capacity to love. You live in the flow of life rather than struggle against it, because like nature, you do not question all the time who you are or where you are going. You simply are.

I came to this conclusion after one incident in particular. It occurred while I was on my morning speed walk, trying to come up with an answer to the question my friend had posed for me: What does it mean to be enlightened? I really did not know.

While deep in thought and speed-walking, I passed an elderly Hasidic Jew who asked me, "Excuse me, miss, tell me, are you Jewish?"

My instant reaction was annoyance, followed quickly by guilt. I realized, though, that I was not sure why the question made me feel negative and threatened. I actually felt angry toward this man. I knew it wasn't fair to respond to this man from a place of fear or anger, so I brought my awareness down into my heart, created my SHIELD, and asked myself the question. To my brain's surprise, I answered him clearly, "No, I am not." He apologized for bothering me and went on.

As I walked away, I was left with so many questions: Why did I respond so negatively to the question? Why so much fear and anger? Why guilt? Why did I say I wasn't Jewish, when I was brought up Jewish? Who am I?

My inner voice told me, "I am me. I am Jewish. I am Hindu. I am Christian. I am Buddhist. I am Spirit. I am One." I realized that to say I am Jewish is to separate myself from the Oneness of everything, to label and categorize myself, as people are accustomed to do in order to feel safe and separated from what they don't know. But by going into my heart, I was fully aware of who I am, fully aware of the Oneness that encompasses all, and that the only reality is love, God, or Spirit. Had the man asked me how my family raised me, in what religion or tradition, then the answer would of course have been different. I was raised in the Jewish tradition. But my interaction with him would have been far less profound.

I asked myself then, Is there any connection between this understanding and my friend's question?

When I arrived home, I sat in meditation and I came to this: On one level, I am the daughter of a Libyan Jew (my father) and an American Jew (my mother). I am the product of my Jewish upbringing. I have lived in Israel. I have studied medicine. I have been healthy and I have been sick. I have loved and I have hated. But who am I, really? Am I not more than the sum of my experiences; am I not more than the product of my upbringing?

ME: Who am I?

INNER VOICE: A fish.

ME: A fish! What do you mean "a fish"?

INNER VOICE: A fish. A fish is a damn fish. (Yes, my inner voice used a swearword. Go figure.) It doesn't question the fact that it is a fish. Humans, they question everything! A fish, no, it is just a fish. It follows its instincts. It knows when to move with the current, how to flow with the comings and goings of the sea. It doesn't try to be a turtle. It doesn't try to be thin. It just does what it does. It is what it is. A fish is a damn fish.

ME: Oh.

I let it sink in a bit, then:

ME: Ooooooooh. I have to love myself as I am. Be connected to all things. I have to learn not to worry or fear so much, to be present and aware, and to use my intuition and instincts.

Curious, I looked up what the symbol of fish represented, and discovered that it represents love, compassion, flow, acceptance, and fertility. I then understood the answer to my friend's question, What does it mean to be enlightened?

In order to live your life in flow, to know who you are, you want to open your heart and fill it with love. You want to create a cushion of love so that you can feel connected to all things and all beings, including yourself, so that when you're under stress, you will know that you have the resources to handle anything; so that when you're under stress, which is almost all the time, rather than activating the Fear Response, you can activate the Love Response; so that rather than feeling separate and alone and consequently instigating negative behaviors and actions that are hurtful to you and others, you feel connected and safe so that your behaviors and actions are helpful to you and others. Ultimately, you do not seek approval and validation from external sources because you feel comfortable in your own body and accept yourself as you are.

So here I am, the fish who was brought up Jewish, trained in Western medicine, and went on to study other healing modalities; who went through pain and depression and self-hatred and came through it happier and healthier; knowing that I am loved and able to fully give love, to share with you all that I know because I want you to learn how to shift into positive physiology, and to be happy and healthy. To become a fish like me. I want you to know who you are and to know you are loved, too.

I am a fish, swimming in the great Oneness of life, offering you the secret of how to heal with love and to live your life in the flow of life.

Come swim with me.

ACKNOWLEDGMENTS

Writing this book has been a wonderful journey for me, enabling me to bring together and pass on to you all that I have learned and experienced. As I write these last sentences, I am in a different place than when I started out with this project. Every patient that I have met with, since the beginning, has taught me more and has enabled me to reflect more about what it means to be healthy and happy. Every new experience I have had has helped me get close to knowing fully who I am and discovering that place of stillness within myself where love resides. Each family member and friend whom I hold dear in my life has continued to remind me what receiving and giving love really means.

Thanks to my wonderful family for being my beacons of support and love. Special thanks to my father, Dr. Jacob Selhub, for being my true mentor and teacher, and to my mother, Shirley Selhub, for being, well, my mother as well as editor, administrative director, and steadfast believer that I could be anything that I wanted to be. Thanks to my siblings, Eliya and Julie Selhub, for loving me no matter how difficult I might have been to live with. And thanks to my wonderful niece, Maia (papaya) Selhub, who continues to teach me how to live my life with an open and joyful heart.

Thanks to my editor, Divina Infusino, for her beautiful writing skills and more important, her friendship. And thanks to my agent, BG Dilworth, for his dedication, perseverance, and loving support. It is because of these two that *The Love Response* has come to your reading eyes.

Thanks to my loving friends, particularly those who supported me through the devastating six months following the HIV needle prick, particularly Dr. Joseph Smiddy and Michelle Pinage, who never left my side. Also thanks to Sharon and Mark Freedman, Dr. Robert Odze, Jonathon Alpert, Peg Baim, Loretta Laroche, Dr. Chiara Piovella, Hari Khalsa, Elina Pechersky, Mia Goldstein, Nira Treidel, Dr. Bindu Raju, and Dr. Suman Reddy for sticking by me as I battled my own demons of depression and loss, and showing me what a Soul Family truly is. And thanks to my dear friend and colleague, Rebecca Lovejoy, who continues to be my "phone buddy," listening and talking to me as we support one another in our quest for knowledge and growth.

My deepest thanks to my German Soul Family, Professor Dr. Gustav Dobos, Karen von-Kleist Dobos, their two daughters Aniko and Marika, Dr. Anna Paul, Nils Altner, Paul Rothenfusser, and the staff at the Clinic for Internal and Integrative Medicine at the Hospital Kliniken Essen-Mitte for embracing *The Love Response* and encouraging me to bring this work to the whole world.

Thanks to the team at Ballantine Books, especially Marnie Cochran, for their support and belief that *The Love Response* was the book everyone would benefit from reading.

Thanks to the staff at the Benson Henry Institute for Mind/Body Medicine at the Massachusetts General Hospital for your encouragement and for your continued dedication to bringing mind/body medicine into the Western medical model.

Lastly, a deep and loving thank-you to all my wonderful patients who allowed me to participate in their path to wellness. You have called me your teacher, but you have truly been mine. You have been my real gurus, as you have brought light into darkness for me.

NOTES

1. Fear: The Ultimate Silent Killer

1. E. A. Phelps and J. E. LeDoux, "Contributions of the amygdala to emotion processing: from animal models to human behavior," *Neuron* 48 (2005): 175–187.
2. G. P. Chrousos and P. W. Gold, "The concepts of stress and stress system disorders. Overview of physical and behavioral homeostasis," *Journal of the American Medical Association* 267 (1992): 1244–1252.
3. E. Charmandari, C. Tsigos, and G. P. Chrousos, "Endocrinology of the stress response," *Annual Review of Physiology* 67 (2005): 258–284. D. S. Charney, "Psychobiological mechanisms of resilience and vulnerability: implications for successful adaptation to extreme stress," *American Journal of Psychiatry* 161(2) (2004): 195–216. I. J. Elenkov and G. P. Chrousos, "Stress system—organization, physiology and immunoregulation," *Neuroimmunomodulation* 13(5–6) (2006): 257–267. K. E. Habib, P. W. Gold, and G. P. Chrousos, "Neuroendocrinology of stress," *Endocrinology Metabolism Clinics of North America* 30 (2001): 695–728. B. S. McEwen and J. C. Wingfield, "The concept of allostasis in biology and medicine," *Hormones and Behavior* 43 (2003): 2–15.
4. I. C. Chikanza, P. Petrou, G. Kingsley, G. Chrousos, and G. S. Panayi, "Defective hypothalamic response to immune and inflammatory stimuli in patients with rheumatoid arthritis," *Arthritis and Rheumatism* 35 (1992): 1281–1288. Elenkov and Chrousos, "Stress system."
5. Chrousos and Gold, "The concepts of stress and stress system disorders." Charmandari et. al., "Endocrinology of the stress response."

M. A. Demitrack and L. J. Crofford, "Evidence for and pathophysiologic implications of hypothalamic-pituitary-adrenal axis dysregulation in fibromyalgia and chronic fatigue syndrome," *Annals of the New York Academy of Sciences* 840 (1998): 684–697. A. N. Vgontzas, E. O. Bixler, and G. P. Chrousos, "Obesity-related sleepiness and fatigue: the role of the stress system and cytokines," *Annals of the New York Academy of Sciences* 1083 (2006): 329–344. I. J. Elenkov, D. G. Iezzoni, A. G. Harris, and G. P. Chrousos, "Cytokine dysregulation, inflammation and well-being," *Neuroimmunomodulation* 12(5) (2005): 255–269.

2. FEAR: A LACK OF LOVE

1. S. E. Taylor, J. S. Lerner, R. M. Sage, B. J. Lehman, and T. E. Seeman, "Early environment, emotions, responses to stress, and health," *Journal of Personality* 72(6) (2004): 1365–1394.

2. R. J. Davidson, D. C. Jackson, and N. H. Kalin, "Emotion, plasticity, context and regulation: perspectives from affective neuroscience," *Psychological Bulletin* 126(6) (2000): 890–909.

3. D. Francis and M. J. Meaney, "Maternal care and development of stress responses," *Current Opinions in Neurobiology* 9 (1999): 128–134.

4. R. L. Repetti, S. E. Taylor, and T. E. Seeman, "Risky families: family social environments and the mental and physical health of offspring," *Psychological Bulletin* 128(2) (2002): 330–336.

5. Repetti, Taylor, and Seeman, "Risky families." S. E. Taylor, B. M. Way, W. T. Welch, J. H. Clayton, B. J. Lehman, and N. I. Eisenberger, "Early family environment, current adversity, the serotonin transporter polymorphism and depressive symptomatology," *Biological Psychiatry* 60 (2006): 671–676.

6. Repetti, Taylor, and Seeman, "Risky families."

7. Taylor et al., "Early family environment." S. Herbst, R. H. Pietrzak, J. Wagner, W. B. White, and N. M. Petry, "Lifetime major depression is associated with coronary heart disease in older adults: results from the National Epidemiologic Survey on Alcohol and Related Conditions," *Psychosomatic Medicine* 69(8) (2007): 729–734.

8. M. J. Knol, J. W. Twisk, A. T. Beekman, R. J. Heine, F. J. Snoek, and F. Pouwer, "Depression as a risk factor for the onset of type 2 diabetes mellitus. A meta-analysis," *Diabetologia* 49(5) (2006): 837–845.

9. L. V. Doering, O. Martínez-Maza, D. L. Vredevoe, and M. J. Cowan, "Relation of depression, natural killer cell function, and infections after coronary artery bypass in women," *European Journal of Cardiovascular Nursing* 7(1) (2008): 52–58.

10. A. Székely, P. Balog, E. Benkö, T. Breuer, J. Székely, M. D. Kertai, F. Horkay, M. S. Kopp, and J. F. Thayer, "Anxiety predicts mortality and

morbidity after coronary artery and valve surgery—a 4-year follow-up study," *Psychosomatic Medicine* 69(7) (2007): 625–631. I. Kawachi, D. Sparrow, P. S. Vokonas, and S. T. Weiss, "Symptoms of anxiety and risk of coronary heart disease. The Normative Aging Study," *Circulation* 90(5) (1994): 225–229.

11. T. Q. Miller, T. W. Smith, C. W. Turner, M. L. Guijarro, and A. J. Hallet, "A meta-analytic review of research on hostility and physical health," *Psychological Bulletin* 119(2) (1996): 322–348.

12. J. E. Graham, T. F. Robles, J. K. Kiecolt-Glaser, W. B. Malarkey, M. G. Bissell, and R. Glaser, "Hostility and pain are related to inflammation in older adults," *Brain, Behavior, and Immunity* 20(4) (2006): 389–400.

3. THE ANTIDOTE TO FEAR: THE LOVE RESPONSE

1. A. Bartels and S. Zeki, "The neural correlates of maternal and romantic love," *Neuroimage* 21(3) (2004): 1155–1166.

2. T. Esche and G. B. Stefano, "The neurobiology of love," *Neuroendocrinology Letters* 26(3) (2005): 175–192. T. Esche and G. B. Stefano, "Love promotes health," *Neuroendocrinology Letters* 26(3) (2005): 264–268.

3. A. Székely, P. Balog, E. Benkö, T. Breuer, J. Székely, M. D. Kertai, F. Horkay, M. S. Kopp, and J. F. Thayer, "Anxiety predicts mortality and morbidity after coronary artery and valve surgery—a 4-year follow-up study," *Psychosomatic Medicine* 69(7) (2007): 625–631.

4. J. Winberg, "Mother and newborn baby: mutual regulation of physiology and behavior—selective review," *Developmental Psychobiology* 46(3) (2005): 217–229.

5. Esche and Stefano, "The neurobiology of love." Esche and Stefano, "Love promotes health."

6. K. C. Light, K. M. Grewen, and J. A. Amico, "More frequent partner hugs and higher oxytocin levels are linked to lower blood pressure and heart rate in premenopausal women," *Biological Psychology* 69(1) (2005): 5–21.

7. K. M. Grewen, B. J. Anderson, S. S. Girdler, and K. C. Light, "Warm partner contact is related to lower cardiovascular reactivity," *Behavioral Medicine* 29(3) (2003): 123–130.

8. A. Marschner, T. Mell, I. Wartenburger, A. Villringer, F. M. Reischies, and H. R. Heekeren, "Reward-based decision-making and aging," *Brain Research Bulletin* 67(5) (2005): 382–390.

9. J. Pearce, *Evolution's End: Claiming the Potential of Our Intelligence* (New York: Harper & Row, 1992).

10. G. Ostir, K. S. Markides, S. A. Black, and J. S. Goodwin, "Emotional well-being predicts subsequent functional independence and survival," *Journal of the American Geriatrics Society* 48(5) (2000): 473–478.

11. A. Steptoe, J. Wardle, and M. Marmot, "Positive affect and health-related neuroendocrine cardiovascular, and inflammatory processes," *Proceedings of the National Academy of Sciences* 102(18) (2005): 6508–6512.

12. L. S. Richman, L. Kubzansky, and J. Maselko, "Positive emotion and health: going 'beyond the negative,' " *Health Psychology* 24(4) (2005): 422–429.

5. BUILDING YOUR LOVE PYRAMID: SOCIAL LOVE

1. D. Spiegel, J. R. Bloom, H. C. Kraemer, and E. Gottheil, "Effect of psychosocial treatment on survival of patients with metastatic breast cancer," *Lancet* 14(2) (8668) (1989): 888–891.

2. X. Zhang, S. L. Norris, E. W. Gregg, and G. Beckles, "Social support and mortality among older persons with diabetes," *Diabetes Education* 33(2) (2007): 273–281.

3. W. Lauder, K. Mummery, M. Jones, and C. Caperchione, "A comparison of health behaviours in lonely and non-lonely populations," *Psychology Health and Medicine* 11(2) (May 2006): 233–245.

4. J. K. Kiecolt-Glaser, T. J. Loving, J. R. Stowell, W. B. Malarkey, S. Lemeshow, S. L. Dickinson, and R. Glaser, "Hostile marital interactions, proinflammatory cytokine production, and wound healing," *Archives of General Psychiatry* 62(12) (2005): 1377–1384.

5. J. S. Odendaal and R. A. Meintjes, "Neurophysiological correlates of affiliative behaviour between humans and dogs," *Veterinary Journal* 165(3) (2003): 296–301.

6. K. Allen, J. Blascovich, and W. B. Mendes, "Cardiovascular reactivity and the presence of pets, friends, and spouses: the truth about cats and dogs," *Psychosomatic Medicine* 64(5) (2002): 727–739.

7. J. Jorgenson, "Therapeutic use of companion animals in health care," *Image: Journal of Nursing Scholarship* 29(3) (1997): 249–254.

8. H. M. Hendy, "Effects of pet and/or people visits on nursing home residents," *International Journal of Aging and Human Development* 25(4) (1987): 279–291.

9. J. M. Siegel, "Stressful life events and use of physician services among the elderly: the moderating role of pet ownership," *Journal of Personality and Social Psychology* 58(6) (1990): 1081–1086.

8. THE LOVE PYRAMID: BUILDING SELF-LOVE

1. J. Crocker, "The costs of seeking self-esteem," *Journal of Social Issues* 58(3) (2002): 597–615.

2. D. C. Reitzes and E. J. Mutran, "Self and health: factors that encourage self-esteem and functional health," *Journal of Gerontology: Series B: Psychological Sciences and Social Sciences* 61(1) (2006): S44-S51.

3. T. L. Gruenewald, M. E. Kemeny, N. Aziz, and J. L. Fahey, "Acute threat to the social self: shame, social self esteem, and cortisol activity," *Psychosomatic Medicine* 6 (2004): 915–924.
4. M. Shimizu and B. W. Pelham, "The unconscious cost of good fortune: implicit and explicit self-esteem, positive life events, and health," *Health Psychology* 23(1) (2004): 101–105.
5. Ibid.

11. COMPLETING THE LOVE PYRAMID: SPIRITUAL LOVE

1. M. Jantos and H. Kiat, "Prayer as medicine: how much have we learned?" *The Medical Journal of Australia* 186 (10 suppl.) (2007): S51–S53. H. Benson, *The Relaxation Response* (New York: William Morrow and Co., 1975).
2. J. D. Kark, G. Shemi, Y. Friedlander, O. Martin, I. Manor, and S. H. Blondheim, "Does religious observance promote health? Mortality in secular and religious kibbutzim in Israel," *American Journal of Public Health* 86 (1996): 341–346. H. G. Koenig, *Is Religion Good for Your Health? Effects of Religion on Physical and Mental Health* (New York: Haworth Press, 1997).
3. R. F. Gillum and D. D. Ingram, "Frequency of attendance at religious services, hypertension, and blood pressure: the Third National Health and Nutrition Examination Survey," *Psychosomatic Medicine* 68(3) (2006): 382–385.
4. A. H. Harris and C. E. Thoresen, "Volunteering is associated with delayed mortality in older people: analysis of the longitudinal study of aging," *Journal of Health Psychology* 10(6) (2005): 739–752.
5. S. Brown, R. M. Nesse, A. D. Vonokur, and D. M. Smith, "Providing social support may be more beneficial than receiving it: results from a prospective study of mortality," *Psychological Science* 14(4) (2003): 320–327.
6. A. Luks, "Helper's high: volunteering makes people feel good, physically and emotionally," *Psychology Today* 22(10) (October 1988): 39–42.
7. E. M. Sternberg, "Approaches to defining mechanisms by which altruistic love affects health" (Shaker Heights, OH: Institute for Research on Unlimited Love, 2005).
8. S. Post, "Altruism, happiness, and health: it's good to be good," *International Journal of Behavioral Medicine* 12(2) (2007): 66–77.

REFERENCES

STRESS/FEAR RESPONSE SYSTEM PHYSIOLOGY

Bergh, F. T., Kumpfel, T., Trenkwalder, C., Rupprecht, R., and Holsboer, F. "Dysregulation of the hypothalamo-pituitary-adrenal axis is related to the clinical course of MS." *Neurology* 53: 772.

Cacioppo, J. T., Berntson, G., Gary G., Malarkey, W. B., Kiecolt-Glaser, J. K., Sheridan, J. F., Poehlmann, K. M., Burleson, M. H., Ernst, J. M., Hawkley, L. C., and Glaser, R. "Autonomic, neuroendocrine and immune responses to psychological stress: the stress reactivity hypothesis," *Annals of the New York Academy of Sciences,* 1:840 (1998): 664–673.

Charmandari, E., Tsigos, C., and Chrousos, G. P. "Endocrinology of the stress response." *Annual Review of Physiology* 67 (2005): 258–284.

Charney, D. S. "Psychobiological mechanisms of resilience and vulnerability: implications for successful adaptation to extreme stress." *American Journal of Psychiatry* 161(2) (2004): 195–216.

Chikanza, I. C., Petrou, P., Kingsley, G., Chrousos, G. P., and Panayi, G. S. "Defective hypothalamic response to immune and inflammatory stimuli in patients with rheumatoid arthritis." *Arthritis and Rheumatism* 35 (1992): 1281–1288.

Chrousos, G. P. "The hypothalamic-pituitary-adrenal axis and immune-mediated inflammation." *New England Journal of Medicine* 332 (1995): 1351–1362.

Chrousos, G. P., and Gold, P. W. "The concepts of stress and stress system disorders. Overview of physical and behavioral homeostasis." *Journal of the American Medical Association* 267 (1992): 1244–1252.

Demitrack, M. A., and Crofford, L. J. "Evidence for and pathophysiologic implications of hypothalamic-pituitary-adrenal axis dysregulation in fibromyalgia and chronic fatigue syndrome."*Annals of the New York Academy of Sciences* 840 (1998): 684–697.

Elenkov, I. J., and Chrousos, G. P. "Stress system—organization, physiology and immuno-regulation," *Neuroimmunomodulation* 13(5–6) (2006): 257–267.

Habib, K. E., Gold, P. W., and Chrousos, G. P. "Neuroendocrinology of stress," *Endocrinology Metabolism Clinics of North America* 30 (2001): 695–728.

Kamal, E. H., Gold, P. W., and Chrousos, G. P. "Neuroendocrinology of stress." *Neuroendocrinology* 30 (2001): 695–728

McEwen, B. S., and Wingfield, J. C. "The concept of allostasis in biology and medicine." *Hormones and Behavior* 43 (2003): 2–15.

Amygdala and Hippocampus

McEwen, B. S. "Plasticity of the hippocampus: adaptation to chronic stress and allostatic load." *Annals of the New York Academy of Sciences* 933 (2001): 265–277.

Phelps, E. A., and LeDoux, J. E. "Contributions of the amygdala to emotion processing: from animal models to human behavior." *Neuron* 48 (2005): 175–187.

Memory, Processing, Assumptions, and Predictions

Caldu, X., and Dreher, J. C. "Hormonal and genetic influences on processing reward and social information." *Annals of the New York Academy of Sciences* 1118 (2007): 43–73.

Dehaene, S., and Changeux, J. P. "Reward-dependent learning in neuronal networks for planning and decision making." *Progress in Brain Research* 126 (2000): 217–229.

Pally, R. "The predicting brain: unconscious repetition, conscious reflection and therapeutic change." *International Journal of Psychoanalysis* 88 (pt. 4) (2007): 861–881.

Thagard, P., and Aubie, B. "Emotional consciousness: a neural model of how cognitive appraisal and somatic perception interact to produce qualitative experience." *Consciousness and Cognition* (2007): 1–17.

Weller, J. A., Levin, I. P., Shiv, B., and Bechara, A. "Neural correlates of adaptive decision making for risky gains and losses." *Psychological Science* 18(11) (2007): 958–964.

Yacubian, J., Glascher, J., Schroeder, K., Sommer, T., Braus, D. F., and

Buchel, C. "Dissociable systems for gain-and-loss-related value predictions and errors of prediction in the human brain." *Journal of Neuroscience* 26(37) (2006): 9530–9537.

THE IMMUNE SYSTEM

Chrousos, G. P. "Therapeutic and clinical implications of systemic allergic inflammation. Stress, chronic inflammation, and emotional and physical well-being: concurrent effects and chronic sequelae." *Journal of Allergy and Clinical Immunology* 106 (2000): S275–S291.

Das, U. N. "Is obesity an inflammatory condition?" *Nutrition* 17 (2001): 953–966.

Dhabhar, F. S. "Stress-induced enhancement of cell-mediated immunity." *Annals of the New York Academy of Sciences* 8400 (1998): 359–372.

Elenkov, I. J., Iezzoni, D. G., Harris, A. G., and Chrousos, G. P. "Cytokine dysregulation, inflammation and well-being." *Neuroimmunomodulation Review* 12(5) (2005): 255–269.

Esche, T., and Stefano, G. B. "Proinflammation: A common denominator or initiator of different pathophysiological disease processes." *Medical Science Monitor* 8 (2002): HY1–HY9.

Esche, T., Stefano, G. B., Fricchione, G. L., and Benson, H. "An overview of stress and its impact in immunological diseases." *Modern Aspects of Immunobiology* 2 (2002): 187–192.

EMOTIONS AND AFFECT

Davidson, R. J. "Well-being and affective style: neural substrates and biobehavioural correlates." *Philosophical Transactions of the Royal Society of London* B, 359 (2004): 1395–1411.

Davidson, R. J., Jackson, D. C., and Kalin, N. H. "Emotion, plasticity, context and regulation: perspectives from affective neuroscience." *Psychological Bulletin* 126(6) (2000): 890–909.

Fredrickson, B. "What good are positive emotions?" *Review of General Physiology* 2(3) (1998): 300–319.

LeDoux, J. *The Emotional Brain.* New York: Simon and Schuster, 1996.

Ostir, G., Markides, K. S., Black, S. A., and Goodwin, J. S. "Emotional well being predicts subsequent functional independence and survival." *Journal of the American Geriatrics Society* 48(5) (2000): 473–478.

Richman, L. S., Kubzansky, L., and Maselko, J. "Positive emotion and health: going 'beyond the negative.' " *Health Psychology* 24(4) (2005): 422–429.

Steptoe, A., Wardle, J., and Marmot, M. "Positive affect and health-related neuroendocrine cardiovascular, and inflammatory processes." Proceedings of the *National Academy of Sciences* 102(18) (205): 6508–6512.

The Childhood Factor

Boccia, M. L., and Pedersen, C. A. "Brief vs. long maternal separations in infancy: contrasting relationships with adult maternal behavior and lactation levels of aggression and anxiety." *Psychoneuroimmunology* 26 (2001): 657–672.

Chen E., Bloomberg, G. R., Fisher, E. B., Jr., and Strunk, R. C. "Predictors of repeat hospitalizations in children with asthma: the role of psychosocial and socioenvironmental factors." *Health Psychology* 22(1) (2003): 12–18.

Davey, C. G., Yucel, M., and Allen, N. B. "The emergence of depression in adolescence: development of the prefrontal cortex and the representation of reward." *Neuroscience Biobehavior Review* 32 (2008): 1–19.

Fenoglio, K. A., Chen, Y., and Baram, T. Z. "Neuroplasticity of the hypothalamic-pituitary-adrenal axis early in life requires recurrent recruitment of stress-regulating brain regions." *Journal of Neuroscience* 26(9) (2006): 2434–2442.

Francis, D., Champagne, F. A., Liu, D., and Meaney, M. J. "Maternal care, gene expression, and the development of individual differences in stress reactivity." *Annals of the New York Academy of Sciences* 896 (1999): 66–84.

Francis, D., Diorio, J., Liu, D., and Meaney, M. J. "Nongenomic transmission across generations of maternal behavior and stress responses in the rat." *Science* 286(5442) (1999): 1155–1158.

Francis, D., and Meaney, M. J. "Maternal care and development of stress responses." *Current Opinions in Neurobiology* 9 (1999): 128–134.

Herlenius, E., and Lagercrantz, H. "Neurotransmitters and neuromodulators during early human development." *Early Human Development* 65 (2001): 21–37.

McEwen, B. S. "From molecules to mind. Stress, individual differences, and the social environment." *Annals of the New York Academy of Sciences* 935 (2001): 42–49.

Repetti, R. L., Taylor, S. E., and Seeman, T. E. "Risky families: family social environments and the mental and physical health of offspring." *Psychological Bulletin* 128 (2002): 330–336.

Taylor, S. E. "The lifelong legacy of childhood abuse." *American Journal of Medicine* 107 (1999): 399–400.

Taylor, S. E., Lerner, J. S., Sage, R. M., Lehman, B. J., and Seeman, T. E. "Early environment, emotions, responses to stress, and health." *Journal of Personality* 72(6) (2004): 1365–1394.

Taylor, S. E., Way, B. M., Welch, W. T., Calyton, J. H., Lehman, B. J., Eisenberger, N. I. "Early family environment, current adversity, the serotonin transporter polymorphism and depressive symptomatology." *Biological Psychiatry* 60 (2006): 671–676.

Teicher, M. H., Tomoda, A., and Andersen, S. L. "Neurobiological consequences of early stress and childhood maltreatment: are results from human and animal studies comparable?" *Annals of the New York Academy of Sciences* 1071 (2006): 313–323.

Turner-Cobb, J. M. "Psychological and stress hormone correlates in early life: a key to HPA-axis dysregulation and normalization." *Stress* 8(1) (2005): 47–57.

NEGATIVE EMOTIONS AND MOODS AND HEALTH CONSEQUENCES

Boltwood, M. D., Taylor, C. B., Burke, M. B., Grogin, H., and Giacomini, J. "Anger report predicts coronary artery vasomotor response to mental stress in atherosclerotic segments." *American Journal of Cardiology* 72 (1993): 1361–1365.

Doering, L. V., Martínez-Maza, O., Vredevoe, D. L., and Cowan, M. J. "Relation of depression, natural killer cell function, and infections after coronary artery bypass in women." *European Journal of Cardiovascular Nursing* 7(1) (2008): 52–58.

Gold, P. W., and Chrousos, G. P. "Organization of the stress system and its dysregulation in melancholic and atypical depression: high vs. low CRH/NE states." *Molecular Psychiatry* 7 (2002): 254–275.

Goldbourt, U., Yaari, S., and Medalie, J. H. "Factors predictive of long-term coronary heart disease mortality among 10,059 male Israeli civil servants and municipal employees." *Cardiology* 82 (1993): 100–121.

Goldstein, M., and Niaura, R. "Psychological factors affecting physical condition. Cardiovascular disease literature review. Part I: Coronary artery disease and sudden death." *Psychosomatics* 33 (1992): 134–145.

Graham, J. E., Robles, T. F., Kiecolt-Glaser, J. K., Malarkey, W. B., Bissell, M. G., and Glaser, R. "Hostility and pain are related to inflammation in older adults." *Brain, Behavior, and Immunity* 20(4) (2006): 389–400.

Herbert, T., and Cohen, S. "Depression and immunity: A meta-analytic review." *Psychological Bulletin* 113 (1993): 472–486.

Herbst, S., Pietrzak, R. H., Wagner, J., White, W. B., and Petry N. M. "Lifetime major depression is associated with coronary heart disease in older adults: results from the National Epidemiologic Survey on Alcohol and Related Conditions." *Psychosomatic Medicine* 69(8) (2007): 729–34.

Kalmijn, S., Tijhuis, M. A., Geerlings, M. I., Giampaoli, S., Nissinen, A., Grobbee, D. E., and Kromhout, D. "Depressive symptoms as risk factor of cardiovascular mortality in older European men: the Finland, Italy and Netherlands Elderly (FINE) study." *European Journal of Cardiovascular Prevention and Rehabilitation* 13(2) (2006): 199–206.

Kawachi, I., Sparrow, D., Spiro, A., 3rd, Vokonas, P., and Weiss S. T. "A prospective study of anger and coronary heart disease, the Normative Aging Study." *Circulation* 1; 94(9) (1996): 290–295.

Kawachi, I., Sparrow, D., Vokonas, P. S., and Weiss S. T. "Symptoms of anxiety and risk of coronary heart disease, the Normative Aging Study." *Circulation* 90(5) (1994): 225–229.

Kiecolt-Glaser, J. K., McGuire, L., Robles, T. F., and Glaser, R. "Emotions, morbidity, and mortality: new perspectives from psychoneuroimmunology." *Annual Review of Psychology* 53 (2002): 83–107.

Knol, M. J., Twisk, J. W., Beekman, A. T., Heine, R. J., Snoek, F. J., and Pouwer, F. "Depression as a risk factor for the onset of type 2 diabetes mellitus. A meta-analysis." *Diabetologia* 49(5) (2006): 837–845.

McEwen, B. S. "Mood disorders and allostatic load." *Biological Psychiatry* 54 (2003): 200–207.

Meyer, S. E., Chrousos, G. P., and Gold, P. W. "Major depression and the stress system: a life span perspective." *Development and Psychopathology* 13 (2001): 565–580.

Miller, T. Q., Smith, T. W., Turner, C. W., Guijarro, M. L., and Hallet, A. J. "A meta-analytic review of research on hostility and physical health." *Psychological Bulletin* 119(2) (1996): 322–348.

Mittleman, M. A., Maclure, M., Sherwood, J. B., Mulry, R. P., Tofler, G. H., Jacobs, S. C., Friedman, R., Benson, H., and Muller, J. E. "Triggering of acute myocardial infarction onset by episodes of anger." *Circulation* 92 (1995): 1720–1725.

Székely, A., Balog, P., Benkö, E., Breuer, T., Székely, J., Kertai, M. D., Horkay, F., Kopp, M. S., and Thayer, J. F. "Anxiety predicts mortality and morbidity after coronary artery and valve surgery—a 4-year follow-up study." *Psychosomatic Medicine* 69(7) (2007): 625–631.

SOCIAL LOVE AND THE NEUROBIOLOGY OF LOVE

Bartels, A. and Zeki, S. "The neural correlates of maternal and romantic love." *Neuroimage* 21(3) (2004): 1155–1166.

Esche, T. and Stefano, G. B. "The neurobiology of love." *Neuroendocrinology Letters* 26(3) (2005): 175–192.

Esche, T. and Stefano, G. B. "Love promotes health." *Neuroendocrinology Letters* 26(3) (2005): 264-268.

Grewen, K. M., Anderson, B. J., Girdler, S. S., and Light, K. C. "Warm partner contact is related to lower cardiovascular reactivity." *Behavioral Medicine* 29(3) (2003): 123–130.

Light, K. C., Grewen, K. M., and Amico, J. A. "More frequent partner hugs and higher oxytocin levels are linked to lower blood pressure and heart rate in premenopausal women." *Biological Psychology* 69(1) (2005): 5–21.

Marschner, A., Mell, T., Wartenburger, I., Villringer, A., Reischies, F. M., and Heekeren, H. R. "Reward-based decision-making and aging." *Brain Research Bulletin* 67(5) (2005): 382–390.

Pearce, J. *Evolution End: Claiming the Potential of Our Intelligence* (New York: Harper & Row, 1992).

Winberg, J. "Mother and newborn baby: mutual regulation of physiology and behavior—selective review." *Developmental Psychobiology* 46(3) (2005): 217–229.

Social Love and Health

Allen, K., Blascovich, J., and Mendes, W. B. "Cardiovascular reactivity and the presence of pets, friends, and spouses: the truth about cats and dogs." *Psychosomatic Medicine* 64(5) (2002): 727–739.

Hendy, H. M. "Effects of pet and/or people visits on nursing home residents," *International Journal of Aging and Human Development* 25(4) (1987): 279–291.

Jorgenson, J. "Therapeutic use of companion animals in health care." Image: Journal of Nursing Scholarship 29(3) (1997): 249–254.

Kiecolt-Glaser, J. K., Loving, T. J., Stowell, J. R., Malarkey, W. B., Lemeshow, S., Dickinson, S. L., and Glaser, R. "Hostile marital interactions, proinflammatory cytokine production, and wound healing." Archives of *General Psychiatry* 62(12) (2005): 1377–1384.

Lauder, W., Mummery, K., Jones, M., and Caperchione, C. "A comparison of health behaviours in lonely and non-lonely populations." *Psychology Health and Medicine* 11(2) (May 2006): 233–245.

Odendaal, J. S., and Meintjes, R. A. "Neurophysiological correlates of affiliative behaviour between humans and dogs." *Veterinary Journal* 165(3) (2003): 296–301.

Spiegel, D., Bloom, J. R., Kraemer, H. C., and Gottheil, E. "Effect of psychosocial treatment on survival of patients with metastatic breast cancer." *Lancet* 14(2)(8668) (1989): 888–891.

Siegel, J. M. "Stressful life events and use of physician services among the elderly: the moderating role of pet ownership." *Journal of Personality and Social Psychology* 58(6) (1990): 1081–1086.

Zhang, X., Norris, S. L., Gregg, E. W. and Beckles, G. "Social support and mortality among older persons with diabetes." Diabetes Education 33(2) (2007): 273–281.

Self Love and Health

Crocker, J. "The costs of seeking self-esteem." *Journal of Social Issues* 58(3) (2002): 597–615.

Gruenewald, T. L., Kemeny, M. E., Aziz, N., and Fahey, J. L. "Acute threat to the social self: shame, social self esteem, and cortisol activity." *Psychosomatic Medicine* 6 (2004): 915–924.

Reitzes, D. C., and Mutran, E. J. "Self and health: factors that encourage self-esteem and functional health," *Journal of Gerontology: Series B: Psychological Sciences and Social Sciences* 61(1) (2006): S44-S51.

Shimizu, M., and Pelham, B. W. "The unconscious cost of good fortune: implicit and explicit self-esteem, positive life events, and health." *Health Psychology* 23(1) (2004): 101–105.

Spirituality and Health

Benson, H. *The Relaxation Response* (New York: William Morrow and Co., 1975).

Brown, S., Nesse, R. M., Vonokur, A. D., and Smith, D. M. "Providing social support may be more beneficial than receiving it: results from a prospective study of mortality." *Psychological Science* 14(4) (2003): 320–327.

Gillum, R. F., and Ingram, D. D. "Frequency of attendance at religious services, hypertension, and blood pressure: the Third National Health and Nutrition Examination Survey." *Psychosomatic Medicine* 68(3) (2006): 382–385.

Harris, A. H., and Thoresen, C. E., "Volunteering is associated with delaying mortality in older people: analysis of the longitudinal study of aging." *Journal of Health Psychology* 10(6) (2005): 739–752.

Jantos, M., and Kiat, H. "Prayer as medicine: how much have we learned?" *The Medical Journal of Australia* 186 (10 suppl.) (2007): S51–S53.

Kark, J. D., Shemi, G., Friedlander, Y., Martin, O., Manor, I., and Blondheim, S. H. "Does religious observance promote health? Morality in secular and religious kibbutzim in Israel," *American Journal of Public Health* 86 (1996): 341–346.

Koenig, H. G. *Is Religion Good for Your Health? Effects of Religion on Physical and Mental Health* (New York: Haworth Press, 1997).

Luks, A. "Helper's high: volunteering makes people feel good, physically and emotionally." *Psychology Today,* 22(10) (October 1988): 39–42.

Post, S. "Altruism, happiness, and health: it's good to be good." *International Journal of Behavioral Medicine* 12(2) (2007): 66–77.

Sternberg, E. M. "Approaches to defining mechanisms by which altruistic love affects health." (Shaker Heights, OH: Institute for Research on Unlimited Love, 2005).

INDEX

ABOUT THE AUTHOR

EVA M. SELHUB, M. D., is a senior staff physician at the Benson Henry Institute for Mind/Body Medicine at Massachusetts General Hospital. An integrative health specialist and the founder of Alight Medicine for Learning and Healing in Newton, Massachusetts, she is also a clinical instructor of medicine at Harvard Medical School. Dr. Selhub has lectured throughout the United States and Europe and has trained healthcare professionals across the globe. Her articles have been published in medical journals and featured in national publications, including *The New York Times, USA Today, Self, Shape, Fitness,* and *Journal of Woman's Health,* and she has appeared on television in connection with her work. Dr. Selhub lives in Boston.

www.loveresponse.com

ABOUT THE TYPE

This book was set in Sabon, a typeface designed by the well-known German typographer Jan Tschichold (1902–74). Sabon's design is based upon the original letter forms of Claude Garamond and was created specifically to be used for three sources: foundry type for hand composition, Linotype, and Monotype. Tschichold named his typeface for the famous Frankfurt typefounder Jacques Sabon, who died in 1580.